FIRST FOODS

Dr. Miriam Stoppard

FIRST
FOODS

DK PUBLISHING, INC.

A DK PUBLISHING BOOK

DESIGN & EDITORIAL   Mason Linklater

SENIOR MANAGING ART EDITOR   Lynne Brown
MANAGING EDITOR   Jemima Dunne

SENIOR ART EDITOR   Karen Ward
SENIOR EDITOR   Penny Warren
US EDITORS   Jill Hamilton, Iris Rosoff,
Joan Whitman

PRODUCTION   Antony Heller

First American Edition, 1998
2 4 6 8 10 9 7 5 3 1

Published in the United States by
DK Publishing, Inc. 95 Madison Avenue,
New York, New York 10016

Visit us on the World Wide Web at http://www.dk.com

Library of Congress Cataloging-in-Publication Data

Stoppard, Miriam.
First foods / by Miriam Stoppard. -- 1st American ed.
p. cm. -- (DK healthcare series)
Includes index.
ISBN 0-7894-3088-6
1. Children--Nutrition. 2. Infants--Nutrition. 3. Cookery
I. Title.   II. Series.
RJ206.S85   1998
649'.3--dc21
97-48450
CIP

Reproduced by Colourscan, Singapore
and IGS, Radstock, Avon
Printed in Hong Kong by Wing King Tong

CONTENTS

INTRODUCTION 6

C H A P T E R

FEEDING AND NUTRITION 9

C H A P T E R

EVERYDAY MEALS 35

C H A P T E R

SPECIAL OCCASIONS 85

INTRODUCTION

There's no question that a child's diet is important because first foods and tastes form the building blocks for a lifetime of good diet and health. What your child eats shouldn't become an obsession with you, however. If you're anxious about it, mealtimes will become battlegrounds. Remember that babies, like all animals, are self-regulating, so try to be flexible and let your child take the lead – up to a point.

EATING PATTERNS

One of the mistakes parents often make is to impose adult appetites and eating habits on children. Children's appetites are notoriously fickle; they're easily distracted from their food and they may have a fad for certain foods for days or even weeks on end. However, your child will get all the nutrients she needs if you try to think in terms of providing her with a wide variety of foods over a weekly rather than a 24-hour period. Don't get upset when she rejects a meal; she'll probably eat heartily at the next one.

From the time they can feed themselves, most children will want fairly frequent meals or snacks consisting of small amounts of food with different textures and colors. *First Foods* shows you how to arrange meals in cheerful picture-book shapes and patterns; it doesn't take a lot of time and effort but does make foods look appealing. Treat the shapes as a catalog of ideas to encourage your child to enjoy eating, to try new foods, and to have fun at mealtimes.

GUIDELINES TO HELP YOUNG EATERS

It's worth following a few guidelines when trying to tempt young eaters. Pay attention to texture. When children are teething, their gums are very sensitive and they're still learning to use their mouths, teeth, and tongues. Crunchy foods served with soft puréed ones will provide good variety at this stage. Use fruits and vegetables for color as well as for all the different nutrients they supply. With vegetables, choose a cooking method such as steaming or stir-frying as often as you can so they keep their color and flavor, and serve some vegetables raw as chewy instant snacks. Remember to keep portions small so that your child isn't put off by the quantity. Better to give seconds than to have a pile of rejected food. Always let foods cool down before serving, since young children's mouths are particularly sensitive to temperature and can be easily burned.

SOCIABLE FAMILY EATING

Mealtimes should be relaxed, sociable, and enjoyable occasions. It's important to bring an open mind to feeding children so that you don't put undue pressure on them and make mealtimes unhappy. After the initial weaning process, your child should join with family meals whenever possible to establish a pleasant routine and to learn acceptable table behavior by following your good example. But do keep rules and restrictions at mealtimes to a minimum.

Make your life easier by using a plastic bib and putting newspaper or a plastic sheet on the floor and underneath the high chair, so you can quickly clean up jettisoned food after the meal. The sooner you let children feed themselves with fingers or a spoon, the sooner they become adept at getting the food into their mouths without too much mess. This is part of the attraction of finger foods: not only do they encourage independence and learning, they also give you and the rest of the family time to enjoy the meal.

At first, don't expect your child to be able to feed herself an entire meal. Some food is bound to end up on the floor and in the bib and you'll have to help some of the time. Mealtimes will be more fun for you too, however, if you try to allow your child some independence. But never be tempted to leave your child alone when she's eating. It's too quick and easy for a young child to choke, so always be nearby in case something goes down the wrong way.

HEALTHIER EATING HABITS

Preparing food for a young child may mean making some changes in your cooking habits. For example, don't add salt during or after cooking. Adding salt puts a strain on young kidneys and encourages a taste for salt instead of the food's natural flavor. Whenever you serve anything but fresh, raw foods, try to be aware of exactly what you're feeding your child. All the foods in *First Foods* are wholesome and free from artificial additives. Read labels on processed foods carefully and note the order of the ingredients. They're listed by quantity, with the greatest amount first. If water is at the top of the list, water is the main ingredient and the product won't be very nutritious. Also note the salt, sugar, and gluten content of processed foods.

Cutting down on salt, sugar, and saturated fats is a good idea for everyone, so perhaps this is a time in your life when you too can try to eat a more healthy, wholefood-based diet, if you don't already do so. You may be unfamiliar with some of the foods mentioned in this book. Tofu (beancurd) is one example. It can be an ideal food for babies and young children because it supplies a wide range of nutrients quickly and easily. It's tasteless and smooth in texture but when cooked it absorbs other flavors well. Experiment with tofu; you might be pleasantly surprised.

HOW THIS BOOK IS PLANNED

The first part of this book tells you all about weaning your baby and feeding an older baby and toddler, with helpful food preparation dos and don'ts. You'll find information on family and social eating, practical guidelines to nutrition, and help with feeding problems, including food intolerance and allergies. Separate charts suggest when to introduce different foods to your child and give advice on preparing and serving fresh fruits and vegetables.

The second part of the book is full of wonderful ideas for feeding children from nine months old. All the meals are based on finger foods. They're nutritionally balanced and generally made with foods that you'd use and prepare for the rest of the family. Everyday Meals has ideas for breakfast, meals with eggs and cheese, fish, meat, or vegetables, soups, and snacks and picnics, while Special Occasions shows you how to make healthy treats for festivals such as Easter and Christmas, and birthdays. I hope that the combination of fun shapes, nutritious ingredients, and different flavors will make each one of these meals a winner every time, with you, your child, and your whole family.

1

FEEDING AND NUTRITION

Sometime toward the end of six months is a good time to
start to wean your baby onto solid foods. Then, during the
next six months, he'll move on from mere "tastes" of solids
with his milk feedings to three solid meals a day.
An understanding of basic nutrition will help
you give him the food he needs for healthy growth.
Learning to feed himself is an enormous step in your
baby's physical and intellectual development and you
should encourage all his attempts to do so. Always be
flexible and introduce new foods slowly, one at a time, so
that you can identify food that doesn't suit your child.

EQUIPMENT FOR WEANING YOUR BABY

For the first few months of life, breast milk or formula will be your baby's only food, and it will provide him with all the nutrients he needs. You won't be thinking about giving your baby solid food until he is at least four months of age (see p. 12), and even then you'll need very little equipment; a bib and some spoons will do. At first you can feed him on your lap or in an infant chair. Later, when he can sit up by himself, you'll need a high chair to feed him in.

PORTABLE BOOSTER SEATS AND HIGH CHAIRS

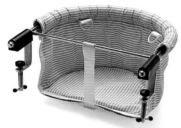

High chair
Many high chairs adapt to other uses, like swings or tables. Make sure that the model you choose is stable and has washable surfaces.

Clip-on chair
This kind of chair is suitable for babies over six months of age. Some models grip the table when the child sits in the chair; others use clamps.

Tray with rim to catch spilled liquids

Stable frame that can be locked in position

Strong restraining strap

Secure safety harness

Booster seat
A child of over 18 months can reach table height with a specially made seat. It is more stable than a cushion and can be firmly strapped to a chair.

Folding model saves space

WHAT YOU WILL NEED TO BUY

To begin with, you'll probably feed your baby on your lap or in an infant seat, but once his neck and back muscles are strong enough to support him (at about six months), a high chair will make life easier. There is a wide choice, and many convert to other uses, such as an all-in-one chair and table for a toddler. Be sure the chair is stable and has washable surfaces, a tray with a rim, and hooks for a safety harness. If you're buying secondhand, check the chair for general wear and tear and see that the surfaces are smooth.

You will also need equipment to mash food into a purée and an unbreakable bowl to serve it in (some come with a suction pad to secure the bowl). Special dishes that keep food hot can be convenient. In addition, you'll need bibs, plastic spoons, forks, and a training cup.

BIBS AND FEEDING UTENSILS

Making the best choice
Choose unbreakable utensils in easy-to-wash plastic. A molded plastic bib with a trough to catch spills is probably most efficient.

OTHER KITCHEN ITEMS

Your kitchen equipment will probably already include the other items you need.

- *A stainless-steel grater with coarse and fine perforations for preparing hard vegetables like carrots before cooking.*

- *A steamer for fast cooking to preserve nutrients. A collapsible model will fit any saucepan.*

- *Nylon chopping boards (not wooden ones, which harbor germs). Prepare vegetables and fruits, raw meats, and cooked meats on separate boards.*

- *A nylon sieve and large plastic, nylon, or stainless-steel spoon, or a small handheld electric blender.*

- *Plastic containers with airtight covers for storing food in the refrigerator.*

Hand-operated food mill
When your baby starts on solids, a hand-operated food mill is a perfectly adequate alternative to a blender for mashing food into a purée.

Fine and coarse cutting disks

FABRIC BIB WITH PLASTIC BACKING

PLASTIC BIB WITH MOLDED TROUGH

PLASTIC BOWL

TRAINING CUP

SPOON AND FORK

WEANING TIPS

Your baby may be reluctant to try new foods, so give him time to get used to each food and don't persist if he seems to dislike something.

• *If your baby doesn't like taking food from a spoon, dip a clean fingertip into the food and let him suck the food off it.*

• *Use unprocessed infant cereals rather than ones that are ready mixed, and make them up in small quantities.*

• *Don't give foods containing nuts, gluten, whole cow's milk, or eggs before six months, to minimize the risk of your child developing later allergies.*

• *Give one new food at a time. Try it once and wait for several days before giving it again to see if there's a reaction.*

WEANING YOUR BABY

Somewhere toward the end of six months is a good time to start to wean your baby onto solid foods. Four months is a little too early, and you could leave it quite a bit later than that. Your baby's young digestive system is incapable of processing, digesting, and absorbing complex foods. If solids are introduced too early, they'll pass through largely undigested, and this will put an increased strain on your baby's immature kidneys.

Milk – either breast milk or its formula equivalent – is the only food that your baby needs in the early months. If a baby is introduced to solids too soon, it can lessen his desire to suck (breast-fed babies will take less milk, and you'll respond by producing less milk). Either way, your baby could end up with a diet that doesn't meet his needs.

WHEN TO WEAN

As your baby grows, he'll need to take in more and more milk to maintain this growth, but his stomach can hold only a certain amount of milk at each feeding. Eventually, he will reach a point where he's drinking to full capacity at each feeding but still doesn't have enough calories for his needs. Your baby will let you know that he needs more to eat by a change in his feeding habits. He may start to demand more milk and appear very unsatisfied after each feeding, or he may start demanding a sixth feeding when he has previously been quite content with five. A classic instance is a baby who has been sleeping through the night starting to wake for a nighttime feeding. This is the time to introduce solids. Many babies do this at around four

SPOONFEEDING

Introducing solid food

Sit your baby in an upright position halfway through his feeding. Scoop up some food on a small spoon and gently insert it between his lips. Don't push the spoon in too far or your baby may gag (he may take a month or two to get used to the spoon). Once your baby has had enough, he will turn his head away.

Messy baby
If your baby pushes out more food than he takes in, gently scrape the excess onto his lips.

months, when their intense desire to suck lessens, although it can be later. You should be aware of the signs that your baby gives you and follow his lead for the introduction of solids. The first tooth, if it appears at or after six months, definitely indicates the need to introduce solid foods.

GIVING THE FIRST SOLIDS

Have a small amount of prepared food ready and then settle in your normal position to feed your baby. Although he is ready for the calories that solid foods provide, your baby will still prefer what he knows to be satisfying – milk. Start by feeding him from one breast or by giving half the usual bottle. Then give him one or two teaspoons of food. Begin with the midday meal because your baby will not be ravenous but will be wide awake and more cooperative. Never force him to take more food than he wants. When he's taken the solid food, give him the rest of the milk. Once he becomes used to solids, he may prefer to take them first.

As soon as your baby is having solid food in any quantity, he will get thirsty and need water. Start with a half fluid ounce (15 milliliters) of water or very diluted fruit juice between and after feedings and whenever he's thirsty. Avoid all sweetened drinks. Aim to give no more than 4½ fluid ounces (120 milliliters) of water and juice a day.

VEGETARIAN WEANING

A growing baby can get all the nutrients necessary for health and vitality from a diet that excludes meat, fish, and poultry provided a proper balance of the different food groups is maintained.

- *Your baby's main source of calories will still be milk, so give this at each feeding.*

- *Cereals and grains provide both carbohydrates and protein for energy and growth, while vegetables and fruits supply essential vitamins and minerals.*

- *A vegetarian diet is bulkier and lower in calories than one with meat, so your baby may get full before he's taken all he needs. To avoid this, make sure to offer a wide variety of low-fiber foods such as cheese.*

EXAMPLES OF WEANING STAGES

FEEDINGS	DAYS 1–4	DAYS 5–8	DAYS 9–12
FIRST	Breast or bottle feeding.	Breast or bottle feeding.	No early a.m. feeding.
SECOND	Half breast or bottle feeding. Try one or two teaspoons of purée or cereal and then give rest of feeding.	Half breast or bottle feeding. Two teaspoons of cereal or baby rice. Rest of feeding.	Half breast or bottle feeding. Two teaspoons of cereal or baby rice. Rest of feeding.
THIRD	Breast or bottle feeding.	Half breast or bottle feeding. Two teaspoons of vegetable or fruit purée. Rest of feeding.	Half feeding. Two teaspoons each of vegetable and fruit purée. Rest of feeding.
FOURTH	Breast or bottle feeding.	Breast or bottle feeding.	As above, but with only two teaspoons of purée.
FIFTH	Breast or bottle feeding.	Breast or bottle feeding.	Breast or bottle feeding.

FIRST TASTES

The chart below is designed to give you an idea of when to introduce different foods to your child. The ages listed are approximate, since children develop at different rates and have individual tastes. Always be flexible and use the chart as a guide only. Introduce new foods slowly, one at a time, so that you can identify food that doesn't suit your baby. If

APPROXIMATE AGES FOR INTRODUCING DIFFERENT FOODS TO YOUR CHIL

FOOD	3–6 MONTHS	4–6 MONTHS	6–7 MONTHS
CEREALS	Fortified baby cereal	Nonwheat cereals, rice, oats, millets, barley, rye, soy. Cook in twice the volume of liquid	Wheat cereals, muesli, wheat products, bread, crispbr hard teething biscuits
DRINKS	Water, apple juice	Fruit and vegetable juices, well diluted	Whole milk
VEGETABLES	Not yet	Cooked carrots, peas, beans, rutabaga, squash, celery, cauliflower, spinach, parsnip	Tomatoes (peeled or mashed tc a pulp at first) Potatoes (in addition to, not in place of, other vegetables)
FRUITS	Not yet	Cooked fruits, e.g., apples, pears Ripe banana	Soaked dried apricots and othe dried fruits (but avoid raisins)
DAIRY PRODUCTS	Not yet	Not yet	Whole milk Cottage, soft, and hard cheeses Yogurt, plain or with puréed fr
MEAT	Not yet	Not yet	White meat: chicken, turkey Liver: chicken, calves', or lamb'
LEGUMES	Not yet	Not yet	Tofu, lentils, peas
FISH	Not yet	Not yet	White fish, skinned and boned
EGGS	Not yet	Not yet	Egg yolk only
SEEDS, NUTS	Not yet	Not yet	Not yet
LIMIT THESE FOODS		All sweetened drinks	All sweetened drinks

your child rejects any new food, go back to serving his old favorites and try offering him the new food again after a few days. There's no need to insist that your child finishes the new food if he doesn't like it.

As long as you serve a variety of foods from the categories listed below, you will be providing a good range of essential nutrients. Just try to ensure that your child eats foods from each of the food groups (see p. 26) over weekly periods.

KEY TO CHART

Blend or purée
Mash or mince
Soft pieces; finger foods
Larger chopped pieces; finger foods

-9 MONTHS	9–12 MONTHS	OVER 12 MONTHS
hole grains sta (from 8 months)	Wheatgerm	Once child can chew well, bread containing whole grains, e.g., seven-grain bread
ilkshakes	No new foods	No new foods
w vegetable pieces. rve in large chunks at first avoid bits breaking off and ing swallowed whole	More strongly flavored vegetables, e.g., broccoli, cabbage, leeks, onions, peppers	Salad leaves Corn
w, ripe fruits, peeled and ·ded	Raisins, soaked until soft (from 10 months)	Once child can chew well, leave skin on Berries, small seed fruits
ilkshakes ozen yogurt	No new foods	No new foods
an red meat: lamb or beef	Meatballs, meat loaf, beef burger	Well-cooked pork without fat Processed meats, e.g., sausages
ft beans (from 8 months)	No new foods	No new foods
) new foods	Canned fish, well drained Oily fish, e.g., mackerel, tuna	Shellfish Smoked fish
) new foods	Whole egg, whole egg products, e.g., custard (from 10 months)	No new foods
lyunsaturated oils	No new foods	Whole nuts only after 3 years
kes, cookies, fried foods l sweetened drinks	Butter, cream, ice cream All sweetened drinks	Processed meats, honey, candy All sweetened drinks

FEEDING AN OLDER BABY

During his first year, your baby will move on from "tastes" of solids with his milk feedings to three solid meals a day, plus drinks of water, diluted fruit juice, or plain milk.

Once he is happy with two or three different solids, it is important to introduce a variety of tastes and textures. In addition to being able to deal with puréed, mashed, or chopped foods, he'll also learn to enjoy chewing and sucking on larger chunks of food (see p. 18). It is important to remember that every baby has different needs and tastes. If you are in any doubt, just feed him as much as he will take happily. The amount of milk he requires will decrease as the number of solid meals he takes increases. Since he'll be getting most of his calories from solids rather than from milk, your baby will become thirsty. When he does, give him plain water or diluted fruit juice to drink rather than milk. Nonetheless, most babies like to have a milk drink last thing at night until into their second year.

FEEDING YOUR CHILD

Until your baby is six months old, you will probably feed him on your lap or in an infant chair, but once his neck and back muscles are strong enough for him to sit up, you may consider using a high chair or feeding table. With a feeding table, you will have to bend down to feed your baby until he can feed himself. At first you may have to prop him up with cushions, so a high chair is probably the better option. For his safety, make sure your baby is properly strapped in at all times. Your child should always be supervised by an adult while he's eating. Almost all children gag on some food at some stage, and it is essential that you react quickly in such a situation. A new texture, taken for the first time, may make him gag simply out of surprise. If he does gag or appear to choke, pat him firmly on the back and encourage him to cough until the food is dislodged. Talk soothingly and gently rub his back, and he'll be more able to swallow the new food.

Your baby will soon look forward to mealtimes as an opportunity to play as well as eat, so feeding will become messier. Place his high chair away from the walls and put newspapers on the floor in case he starts throwing food. Within a month or so of starting solids, your baby will be able to take food from the spoon.

Encourage self-feeding
Allow your child to spoonfeed himself if he can. Choose non-runny foods, such as cereal or thick purées.

Molded plastic bib to catch spills

SELF-FEEDING

Learning to feed himself is an enormous step in your baby's physical and intellectual development, and so you should encourage all his attempts to do so. His manual dexterity and hand/eye coordination will greatly improve with self-feeding, so let him experiment if he shows an interest and be prepared to cope with the mess.

It may be several months before your baby can really feed himself. Help him by giving him foods that will stick to the spoon, such as cereal, or foods he can hold (see below) if he finds using a spoon frustrating. Food will be a plaything, and most will land on the floor rather than in his mouth. The best way to ensure that he gets at least some food is for both of you to have a spoon. Use two spoons of the same color and type so that you can swap your full spoon for his empty one when he has difficulty scooping up the food.

FOODS FOR SELF-FEEDING

Fruit and vegetables	Cereals and grains	Protein
• Any fresh fruit that is easy to hold, such as bananas, cut into chunks or slices with the skin or seeds removed • Vegetables, particularly carrots, cut into sticks or shapes that are easy to grasp (don't cut pieces too small: your baby might choke) • Thick mashed potato	• Small pieces of dried, sugar-free cereal • Little balls of cooked (preferably brown) rice • Pieces of whole-wheat bread or whole-wheat rusks (not bread that incorporates complete whole grains) • Pasta shapes • Hard teething biscuits	• Pieces of soft cheese, such as Gouda • Pieces of toast with cheese • Small pieces of hamburger • Low-fat soft cheese spread on whole-wheat bread • Any meat in small pieces • Filleted fish, such as cod, in firm chunks • Sliced hard-boiled eggs

FINGER FOODS

If your baby has difficulty using a spoon, he will find finger foods easier to handle.

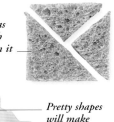

Be sure
bread has
no tough
grains in it

Pretty shapes
will make
food look
appealing

Cut or slice
vegetables
into easy-
to-grasp
shapes

GOOD FOODS

Children's appetites are notably fickle. Children are easily distracted from their food and may eat certain foods for days or even weeks on end. When planning meals for your baby, try not to think in terms of a 24-hour cycle; it's more like a weekly cycle. Don't get upset when he rejects a meal – he will probably eat heartily at the next. Even if he rejects certain foods for weeks at a time, your baby is likely to get the essential nutrients from elsewhere as long as you make sure to serve a wide variety of foods (see p. 26).

Remember, a baby's stomach can't hold very much and he will need to eat more often than you do. Don't insist he finish his meals, and be prepared to give snacks in between. Of course, you should encourage your baby to have regular feeding times, but if you try to make him eat at mealtimes only, meals will become a battleground, and he may end up by not getting the food he needs. The suggested menus below are intended as a guide to your baby's main meals.

SUGGESTED MENUS FOR AN OLDER BABY

MEAL	WITH MEAT	WITHOUT MEAT
BREAKFAST	• Rice cakes • Hard-boiled egg • Breast milk/formula	• Mashed banana • Whole-wheat toast pieces • Breast milk/formula
LUNCH	• Strained vegetables and chicken • Stewed apples (skin and seeds removed) • Diluted fruit juice	• Mashed potato and grated cheese • Pear slices (skin and seeds removed) • Diluted fruit juice
AFTER-NOON	• Whole-wheat toast pieces • Orange segments • Breast milk/formula	• Rice cakes • Apple pieces (skin and seeds removed) • Breast milk/formula
DINNER	• Cauliflower cheese • Semolina with soaked puréed dried fruit such as apricots • Diluted fruit juice	• Pasta shapes with tomato sauce • Yogurt with fruit purée such as mango • Diluted fruit juice

FOODS FOR TEETHERS

When your baby is teething, he will like to chew and suck to soothe his gums. Any piece of raw vegetable or fruit that is large enough to hold easily and can be sucked or chewed makes a good teething food, particularly if it is chilled but not frozen really solid. Whole-wheat crackers give your baby something hard to bite on at first, and then become soft so they can be swallowed easily. If you have time, try to make your own teething biscuits and rusks; they're quick to do, inexpensive, and free from unwanted additives and sugar. Most commercial varieties contain almost as much sugar as ordinary cookies, and those advertised as "low-sugar" simply disguise their sugar content in the form of glucose – not a good start for first teeth. Older children may like to gnaw on a bone, for instance a sparerib, lamb chop, or chicken drumstick, but take care not to offer anything with sharp edges, which can catch on inflamed gums. Teething can be a wearing time for everyone, but try not to resort right away to using medicines and teething gels. Nearly all of them contain a local anesthetic that provides only a moment's relief, and they can also cause allergies.

Relieving the pain
Chewing and sucking on firm-textured foods, such as the ones shown here, help soothe your baby's sore gums and ease the pain of teething.

TEETHING BISCUIT

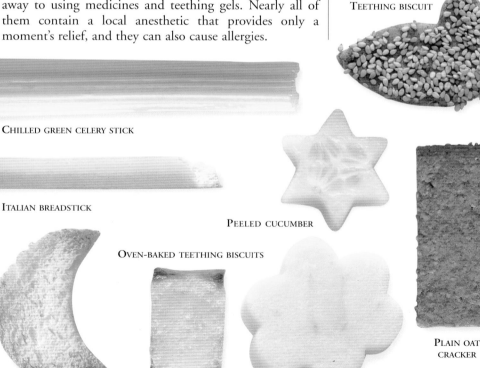

CHILLED GREEN CELERY STICK

ITALIAN BREADSTICK

PEELED CUCUMBER

OVEN-BAKED TEETHING BISCUITS

PLAIN OAT CRACKER

PEELED RAW APPLE

FEEDING YOUR TODDLER

By the age of 18 months, your baby should already be eating more or less the same foods you eat, and will probably take about one-third to half an adult portion at meals. Make sure he has at least one protein food at each meal and four servings of fruits and vegetables a day. Aim to give a good mixture of foods from the different food groups (see p. 28).

Don't give your child highly seasoned or sugary foods; offer nutritious fresh fruit or yogurt rather than sweets. Also avoid any small, hard pieces of food that your child could choke on, such as whole nuts or popcorn, fruits with pits or seeds, or very small pieces of raw fruits or vegetables.

FAMILY EATING

Now that your toddler is feeding himself, he'll enjoy sitting at the table during family mealtimes. Although he's eating the same food as everyone else, you may need to mash or chop it so that he can eat without too much help. A very messy eater can be fed before the rest of the family, then allowed to sit at the table with some finger foods. Difficult eaters feel encouraged to eat more at family meals.

It will be some time, however, before your child is ready to sit still during mealtimes. If he wants to get down from the table, let him go, and don't try to make him come back to finish his food if he has obviously lost interest in it. He will make up for it by eating more at the next meal.

MESSY EATERS

Your child may regard mealtimes as just another game and why not? He'll see nothing wrong in throwing food around, getting it everywhere. Although it may seem that he is doing it on purpose, it's just a phase and his coordination will eventually improve (food provides the perfect motivation for speeding up your child's balance and muscle coordination). To make mealtimes easier and less stressful, spread newspapers under the high chair. You can gather them up at the end of each meal. Being neat can be turned into a game of its own: you could

Keeping clean
Bibs and plastic equipment that is easy to wash help keep messy mealtimes more manageable.

draw a circle on the tray of the high chair to show your toddler where his mug or bowl should go. If he keeps it there, give him a treat or reward (see p. 22).

MENU PLANNING

The menus below assume that your toddler will eat three meals a day and several snacks in between. If you find in practice that he eats fewer meals and more snacks, just make sure you choose snack foods that you would have served at mealtimes, such as Stickman Feast (see p. 77) or Dips (see p. 79) with vegetables, fruits, or crackers.

SUGGESTED MENUS FOR A TODDLER

DAY 1	DAY 2	DAY 3
Breakfast	**Breakfast**	**Breakfast**
½ slice whole-wheat toast	¾oz (25 g) cereal plus ½ cup milk	1 tablespoon baby muesli with 1½ fl oz (50 ml) milk
1 chopped hard-boiled egg	1 sliced pear, no skin	½ mashed banana
1 cup diluted fresh fruit juice	½ slice whole-wheat toast	small pot of fruit yogurt
	1 cup diluted fresh fruit juice	1 cup diluted fresh fruit juice
Lunch	**Lunch**	**Lunch**
1½oz (50 g) white fish	1 beef burger on a whole wheat roll	1 cheese sandwich made with whole wheat bread
1½oz (50 g) brown rice (dry weight)	1oz (30 g) steamed broccoli	pieces of raw carrot
1 tablespoon corn	1 medium tomato	1 sliced apple, no skin
1 cup diluted fresh fruit juice	1 cup diluted fresh fruit juice	1 cup milk
Dinner	**Dinner**	**Dinner**
1½–2½ oz (50–75 g) cauliflower with 1½ oz (50 g) grated cheese	½ whole-wheat roll	2 sardines (packed in brine or tomato sauce, not in oil)
1½oz (50 g) broad beans	1½ oz (50 g) broad beans	1½ oz (50 g) baked beans
1½oz (50 g) chicken, no skin	1½ oz (50 g) chopped liver	1 medium tomato
1 small whole-wheat roll	1½ oz (50 g) whole-wheat pasta (dry weight)	1 cup milk
½ banana blended with 1 cup milk	1 cup water	
Snacks	**Snacks**	**Snacks**
1 small yogurt	1 unsweetened whole-wheat cracker	1 orange in segments
1 banana	1 rice cake	1 fromage frais
1 whole-wheat roll	1 cup water	1 small package potato chips
1 cup water	1 cup milk	1 cup diluted fresh fruit juice

TREATS AND REWARDS

Every parent knows that there are times when it is important either to reward a child's good behavior or offer a bribe in return for some form of cooperation.

Candy might seem like the most suitable reward, since children always appreciate it. However, you may feel that to give candy routinely as a reward undermines the consistency of your approach to candy-eating in general. There is no hard and fast rule on this, and there is no reason why you shouldn't occasionally reward your child with candy as long as you make it clear that it is a one-time gift.

It's worth making an effort, however, to come up with other forms of treat, or reward: a favorite flavor of yogurt, a small toy or new box of crayons, or an especially long bath-time or bedtime story.

I don't believe in placing a total ban on candy, because this can encourage children to become secretive and dishonest.

I do believe in rationing candy, however, and this always worked with my own children. If you let your child have one piece after lunch and one after dinner, and encourage him to brush his teeth afterward, you will be encouraging self-control, good eating habits, and good oral hygiene for his lifetime.

FAMILY AND SOCIAL EATING

For many families, mealtimes are about much more than making sure everyone is fed: they are social occasions when all the members of the family sit down together, exchange news, and enjoy each other's company. For a small child, these times form an important part of his learning process. He can appreciate this social aspect of mealtimes and will learn most of his behavior at the table from his experience of family eating, rather than from lectures on etiquette at a later age. Because of this, the family will be able to enjoy mealtimes without repeated disruptions caused by bad manners and arguments about behavior.

As soon as your child first sat in his high chair at the family dining table, he will have been watching and learning. He will want at least to try the foods that you are eating and will often join in the conversation. Try to include your child in family meals as often as possible. Give praise when he tries to follow your good example; for instance, asking for something to be passed to him instead of attempting to grab it from the other side of the table. Children learn most naturally and easily by example and will rapidly pick up the behavior that the rest of the family exhibits. If everyone in your family leaves the table when it suits him, for example, rather than waiting for the others to finish eating, it will be hard to persuade your child to sit still and wait.

There will be times when you want your child to behave especially well at mealtimes, usually because you are having guests. Allow him to join in the excitement of a special meal by letting him help set the table, perhaps. If he knows that some occasions demand an extra effort, he will find it easier to understand why you want him to be particularly well behaved and will, therefore, react better to your wishes.

KEEPING MEALTIMES RELAXED

It is important that meals don't become a battleground for more generalized family conflict. The association between food and love can be very close, and arguments about food and eating can be associated with tensions over other issues. In such cases, eating behavior, such as a refusal to eat, can become a weapon that the child uses to manipulate you, to gain attention or to express anger, distress, and many other emotions. It is best, therefore, to be fairly easygoing about table etiquette with your child, to keep mealtimes as relaxed as possible, and not to be drawn into arguments. Insist only on those aspects of table manners that you consider to be essential; refinements can come later.

EATING AWAY FROM HOME

An older child will have definite preferences about what he wants to eat and indulge himself. There are likely to be occasions when your child is eating away from home and, while you obviously can't account for every mouthful he eats, it's worth trying to make sure that the good habits he learned at home are not lost once he starts to eat meals elsewhere.

If your child goes to a playgroup, nursery school, or regular school, try to make sure he has a good breakfast beforehand. If he doesn't, he will become hungry long before lunchtime, and both his temper and concentration will be affected. A healthy midmorning snack, for instance, a piece of fruit or breakfast bar, will help tide him over until the next meal. If food is going to be provided for him, try to find out what will be offered. Provide him with a nutritious and healthy packed lunch if you are not happy or if there are no arrangements to feed him. Lunch need not always be sandwiches: try chicken pieces and potato salad, pieces of raw vegetables with a yogurt dip, or other foods that your child can eat with his fingers.

Children are often encouraged to try new foods because they see their friends eat them. You may find once your child starts going to a playgroup or school that he will want to eat foods that he previously rejected at home.

FAST FOODS

When you are out with your child and want to stop for a snack, try not to go to fast food restaurants too often. French fries, hamburgers, hot dogs, and soft drinks are high in salt, fats, and sugar. If you can, take some healthy snack foods with you or choose a place that offers healthier foods, for instance, sandwiches and salads. If your child particularly asks for hamburgers and French fries, however, you may like to indulge him on occasion – but make it clear that such foods are a rare and special treat. My family used to eat at a hamburger restaurant once a week, for Saturday lunch. This satisfied everyone and is not often enough to be unhealthy.

EATING OUT

There will be many occasions when you will want to take your child out to eat. Being prepared will make the experience more enjoyable.

● *Try to find out beforehand what facilities are available at the restaurant you have chosen. If you are reserving a table, tell them that you will be bringing young children, and find out whether there will be room for your child's stroller and whether a high chair can be provided if you need one.*

● *Many children's menus are very limited and offer just hamburgers and hot dogs – both with French fries. If you don't want your child to have these foods, ask whether you can order a small portion of a suitable dish from the main menu, and whether you will be charged full price for it.*

● *Most children will enjoy the experience of eating out, and you should involve your child fully, allowing him to choose his own meal and give his own order to the waiter if he is not too shy.*

● *Take your child's booster seat with you if he normally uses one. If you think he will have difficulty drinking from a glass, you could also take along his training cup.*

● *Many restaurants encourage children and will be happy to provide straws for drinks, bibs, and high chairs for young babies, and even small gifts such as paper to color and crayons for older children.*

OVERWEIGHT

Obesity is one of the most common nutritional problems among children in prosperous Western societies. Most plump children, however, are not medically overweight, and no special action is needed as long as they are healthy and active.

If you think that your child is overweight, consult your doctor, who will know if your child's weight is above the normal range for his height.

Being overweight is most often due to lack of exercise and a poor diet. The best help for the child is often for the whole family to eat a healthier diet – less fat and sugar, more fresh fruits and vegetables, and more unrefined carbohydrates.

Never try to make your child lose weight, but rather keep his weight stable as he grows in height. Try these guidelines:

● *Bake, broil, or boil foods rather than roasting or frying.*

● *Give water or diluted fruit juice, never sweetened drinks, when your child is thirsty.*

● *Give whole-wheat bread, raw vegetables, and fruits as snacks.*

● *Choose whole-wheat – not white – bread, pasta, and rice.*

● *Play lively games with your child to encourage activity.*

● *No child needs more than one pint (500 ml) of milk a day. One or two percent milk is fine for children over one year if vitamin supplements are given in addition.*

FEEDING PROBLEMS

Some young children are "difficult eaters," but in many cases the real difficulty is with a parent who expects the child to conform to an eating pattern that doesn't suit him. If you approach feeding problems with sympathy and a flexible attitude, they will usually just disappear. In some cases, there may be a genuine problem, such as intolerance to certain foodstuffs or an allergy (see p. 27), and you should then consult your doctor. Never attempt to determine and isolate a food allergy on your own.

FOOD PREFERENCES

In the second year, your child will start to show likes and dislikes for certain foods. It is very common for children to go through phases of eating only one kind of food and refusing everything else. For example, he may go for a week eating nothing but yogurt and fruit, then suddenly go right off yogurt and start eating nothing but cheese and mashed potatoes. Don't get angry at your child about this and don't insist that he eats certain foods. No single food is essential to your child, and there is always a nutritious substitute for any food he refuses to eat. As long as you offer your child a wide variety of foods, he will be getting a balanced diet. It is far better for him to eat something that he likes (even if it is something you do not approve of) than to eat nothing at all. The one thing you must watch out for is your toddler refusing to eat all foods from a particular group: refusing fruits or vegetables of any kind, for instance. If he does, his diet will become unbalanced. You will have to think of ways of tempting him to eat fruits and vegetables, perhaps by cooking the food in a different way or by presenting it imaginatively (see pp. 35–93).

If you spend time and effort cooking food that you know your toddler doesn't want, you'll feel annoyed and resentful when he doesn't eat it. Give yourself and your child a break and make life easier on both of you by cooking food that you know he will enjoy.

Don't try to camouflage a disliked food by mixing it with something else, or bargain with your child by offering a favorite food if he eats the disliked one; he may very well end up refusing other foods as well. If you are introducing a new food, make sure your child is hungry. That way, he is more likely to accept it. Never try to force your child to take something that he doesn't want. If he thinks it is very important to you, he will simply use the situation as a way of manipulating you to get what he wants.

REFUSAL TO EAT

Not eating is an early indication that your child may be unwell or unhappy, so observe him carefully. If he looks pale and seems cranky and more clumsy than usual, check his temperature and speak to your doctor if you're worried.

Occasionally, your child may have had a lot of snacks or milk before his meal, and he won't show his usual appetite. As long as the snacks are nutritious, this is nothing to worry about. If he refuses to eat for no reason that you can see, don't let yourself be bothered by it. Your child will always eat as much food as he really needs, and if you insist on him eating, mealtimes may turn into a battle that you will always lose.

FOOD INTOLERANCE

The inability to digest certain foods has to be distinguished from a true food allergy (see p. 27), which is quite different and very rare. Intolerance occurs when the digestive system fails to produce essential enzymes that break down food inside the body. Lactose intolerance – the inability to digest the sugars in cows' milk – is one of the most common forms of food intolerance in children. The enzyme (in this instance lactase) may be absent from birth or its production may have been disrupted by an intestinal disorder, for example, gastroenteritis. Gluten sensitivity, however, is a true allergy (see p. 27) and causes inflammation of the bowel. Smelly, bulky, pale stools are characteristic of the disorder, and you may notice that your child fails to gain weight and appears listless. If he habitually has symptoms such as diarrhea, nausea, or pain after eating a certain food, consult your doctor. The best remedy is just to avoid that food. You'll need expert medical advice to pin down the culprit food and to rule out other possible causes. Gluten sensitivity needs careful medical supervision.

WHEN YOUR CHILD IS SICK

Loss of appetite is often one of the first signs of illness in a child, but this need not be a cause for concern if the illness lasts only a short time.

- *Your child must drink lots of fluids, especially if he has been vomiting or has had diarrhea.*

- *Most doctors recommend that drinks containing milk should be avoided if your child is suffering from gastroenteritis.*

- *There is no need for a special diet, although it is sensible for your child to avoid rich or heavy foods if he has an upset stomach.*

- *Offer some of his favorite foods to cheer him up and give smaller portions than usual. Because your child is resting, he will probably not want to eat very much.*

Good fluid intake
Although your child's appetite may be poor when she is sick, make sure she takes in lots of fluids by offering her favorite drinks.

NUTRITION

Given a free choice, your baby will always take enough food for his needs. If he doesn't want to eat, then he doesn't need to. This means that there will be days when he will eat hardly anything, followed by periods of eating a lot.

To eat a balanced diet, your baby should eat foods from each one of the four different food groups, in roughly the correct proportions (see below). This doesn't have to be on a daily basis, however, so when you are considering whether he is eating well, you need to think in the long term. Look at what he has eaten in the last week, not just in a single day. Viewed like this, a "binge" of eating nothing but bread or potatoes for two days is nothing to worry about, since your baby will probably take in enough fruits and vegetables during the week to balance this out. What is important is that you should be giving him a wide variety of foods to choose from. He can't eat the foods he requires if they are not made available to him.

Your baby will gradually come to eat many of the same foods as you, prepared in a form that he can manage. It would be wrong, however, to suppose that his needs are the same as yours, or that a diet that would be recommended as healthy for you will be good for him. You may try to reduce your fat intake by using low-fat dairy products, for example, but you should give your child whole milk until

The food pyramid
This table identifies the proportions in which the main food groups should be eaten in order for your baby to take in the right balance of nutrients. Carbohydrates and fruits and vegetables are the two most important groups; protein-rich foods such as meat, fish, eggs, dairy products, nuts, and legumes come next. Fats, oils, and sugars should form the smallest part of your baby's diet. The amounts of these that occur naturally in other foods will be more than enough to meet his needs. By following these guidelines for your baby, you will be helping him form good habits for life.

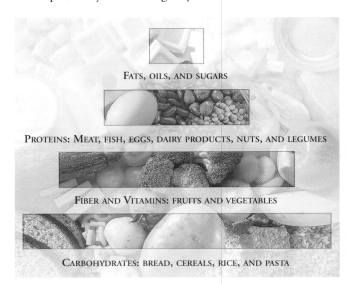

FATS, OILS, AND SUGARS

PROTEINS: MEAT, FISH, EGGS, DAIRY PRODUCTS, NUTS, AND LEGUMES

FIBER AND VITAMINS: FRUITS AND VEGETABLES

CARBOHYDRATES: BREAD, CEREALS, RICE, AND PASTA

he is two years old, unless he is overweight (see p. 24). After that, you can introduce one or two percent milk if you wish. The health benefits of limiting sugar intake, however, apply as much to babies as to adults. In addition, never add salt to your baby's food – his kidneys cannot cope with it.

FOOD ALLERGY

Most cases of suspected food allergy turn out to be no more than intolerance (see p. 25) or the combination of a fussy child and a fussy mother. A true food allergy is quite rare, and occurs when the body's immune system undergoes an exaggerated reaction to a protein or chemical that it interprets as "foreign." Allergy is a protective mechanism of the body, and symptoms can include headache, nausea, profuse vomiting, a rash, widespread red blotches on the skin, and swelling of the mouth, tongue, face, and eyes. The likelihood of your child suffering an allergic reaction is greater if there is a history of allergies in the family.

At first the allergen – which is the substance that causes the reaction – may produce only mild symptoms, but these may become more severe if the child is repeatedly exposed to the food concerned. If you introduce new foods one at a time, with one-week intervals between each introduction, you'll easily recognize any symptoms and be able to consult your doctor. Certain foods like wheat (gluten sensitivity, see p. 25) and egg whites are more likely to cause problems and should be introduced after six months of age. Shellfish, strawberries, nuts, chocolate, and cows' milk also cause allergic reactions. There has been much publicity about sensitivity to food colorings and flavorings as well. In fact, very few children react in an abnormal way as a result of these food additives, but avoid them if you can.

More recent studies have cast doubt on previous claims that food allergies are the cause of behavioral disturbances (including hyperactivity) in children: parents continued to report behavioral disturbance even when the suspect food had been withdrawn from the child's diet, unknown to them. In a very small number of cases, it has been proved that food was responsible for the behavior, but in very many more cases bad behavior is a way of seeking love and attention from neglectful parents. You should never try to isolate a food allergy on your own without expert medical advice and never assume an allergy is present without a clear diagnosis from a pediatric allergist.

FOODS TO AVOID

For safety, you should avoid giving foods that are easy to choke on – that is, small, hard, and easy to swallow, such as peanuts – until your child is 2–3 years old and able to chew well. Other foods that may not be directly harmful to your child but are best limited because they offer very little nutritional value are listed below:

- *Highly sweetened foods (jams, commercial desserts, sweetened condensed milk, cookies, cakes, all candy).*

- *Processed meats (salami, bacon, ham, hot dogs).*

- *Saturated fats (cream).*

- *Canned foods with added salt or sugar (check all labels).*

- *Soda.*

- *Salty foods like potato chips and foods containing hidden salt, such as bouillon cubes.*

A BALANCED DIET

As your child grows, his nutritional requirements increase proportionately: greater quantities of certain nutrients are needed during growth spurts and when he is learning to walk. Your child's diet should contain sufficient amounts of protein, carbohydrates, fats, vitamins, and minerals. He will get all of these as long as you provide a variety of foods. Because he is growing, he still needs more protein and calories for his body weight than an adult.

Generally, eating a range of foods from three of the four food groups – carbohydrates, fruits and vegetables (fiber), and protein-rich foods (see p. 26) – will fulfill your child's needs. However, some foods within the groups have particular nutritional value. All fruits and vegetables provide carbohydrates and fiber, for instance, and leafy vegetables such as cabbage are especially high in minerals, while citrus fruits are a good source of vitamins A and C (see chart).

A good diet is a varied one
Variety is the key to a balanced diet. Choose foods from each of the groups in the chart.

NUTRIENTS FOUND IN DIFFERENT KINDS OF FOODS

FOODS	CONSISTING OF	NUTRIENTS SUPPLIED
BREADS AND CEREALS	Whole-wheat bread, noodles, pasta, rice	Protein, carbohydrates, B group vitamins, iron, calcium
CITRUS FRUITS	Oranges, grapefruits, lemons, limes, tangerines	Vitamins A and C
FATS	Butter, margarine, vegetable oils, fish oils, nut oils	Vitamins A and D, essential fatty acids
GREEN AND YELLOW VEGETABLES	Cabbage, brussels sprouts, spinach, kale, green beans, squash, lettuce, celery, zucchini	Minerals, including calcium, chlorine, fluorine, chromium, cobalt, copper, zinc, manganese, potassium, sodium, magnesium
OTHER VEGETABLES AND FRUITS	Potatoes, beets, corn, carrots, cauliflower, pineapples, apricots, nectarines, peaches, strawberries, plums, apples, bananas	Carbohydrates, vitamins A and C, B group vitamins
HIGH PROTEIN FOODS	Chicken, fish, lamb, beef, pork, eggs, cheese, nuts, legumes	Protein, fat, iron, vitamins A and D, B group vitamins especially B_{12} (naturally present in animal proteins only)
MILK AND DAIRY PRODUCTS	Milk, cream, yogurt, ice cream, cheese	Protein, fat, calcium, vitamins A and D, B group vitamins

SNACKS

Until the age of four or five, your child will prefer to eat often throughout the day. His stomach cannot cope with three adult-sized meals a day, so he is not ready for an adult eating pattern. Typically, he will want to eat five to seven times a day. What he eats is more important than how often he eats. As a rule, the more meals he has, the smaller they will be.

You may be accustomed to thinking of snacks as "extras," but they're an integral part of any child's diet and should not be refused. As long as the snacks do not reduce your child's daily nutrition and are not used as substitutes for "meals," snacks can be useful for introducing new foods gradually without disrupting your child's eating patterns. Avoid giving your child highly refined and processed foods like cookies, candy, cakes, and ice cream, which contain a lot of calories and very few nutrients. Fresh vegetables and fruits, cubes of cheese, cheese sandwiches with whole-wheat bread, and fruit juice all make good, nutritious snacks.

How to plan snacks Snack foods should contribute to the whole day's nutrition, so don't leave them to chance: plan them carefully and coordinate meals and snacks so that you serve different foods in the snacks and in the meals.
• Milk and milk-based drinks make very good snacks and contain protein, calcium, and many of the B group vitamins. You should use whole milk until your child is at least two years old. Then you can use one or two percent milk but not skim milk unless your child is overweight (see p. 24). Raw fruit juices are also nutritious and have a lot of vitamin C. If you buy fruit juice drinks, avoid those with added sugar.
• Since your child may become bored with certain kinds of food, try to give him lots of variety and make snacks amusing and decorative if you can (see pp. 77–84).
• Food that your child rejects in one form may be acceptable to him in another. For instance, yogurt can be frozen so that it becomes more like ice cream. A child who rejects cheese sandwiches might enjoy eating cubes or slices of cheese and tomato pieces out of an ice-cream cone.
• You can also increase your child's interest in food by involving him in planning – or even preparing – part of a snack. He will take great pride in eating a sandwich if he has helped you wash or tear the lettuce, for example, or if you allow him to assemble the bread and filling himself.

Little and often
Your child will need more snacks than you do, since he isn't able to eat large meals.

Scares about food poisoning in recent years have made parents much more conscious of the dangers of poor food hygiene. The commonsense precautions given here will protect your baby.

- *Always wash your hands with soap and hot water before handling food for your baby, especially after using the toilet, changing a diaper, or playing with pets. Make sure your family does the same.*

- *Be scrupulous about keeping the kitchen clean, especially work surfaces, chopping boards, and utensils used in food preparation. Never use wooden utensils: they harbor millions of germs.*

- *Always use a clean dishtowel or paper towels to dry dishes, or let them dry in a rack after rinsing them with hot water.*

- *Keep the kitchen garbage can covered and empty it often. Rinse out the can with hot water and a little disinfectant every time you empty it.*

- *Cover any food that is left out of the cabinet.*

- *Throw away any food that is left over in your baby's bowl.*

FOOD PREPARATION

Once your baby is on solids, it is no longer necessary to sterilize all feeding utensils, although bottles used for milk should still be sterilized until your baby is about nine months old. Cups, bowls, and utensils can be washed in hot, soapy water and rinsed with hot water. Let them dry in a rack or use a clean dishtowel or paper towels. Now that your baby's diet includes a range of foods, however, you need to take precautions to protect him from the effects of harmful bacteria such as salmonella and *E. coli*. You should be well informed about buying, storing, cooking, reheating, and preparing food safely.

BUYING AND STORING

The most important thing to look for when buying food is freshness. Shop often, and use food as quickly as possible. Bruised or damaged fruits and vegetables deteriorate rapidly, so don't buy them. Always wash fruits if the skin is to be eaten, since there may be a residue of insecticides or other chemicals on it. Most processed foods now carry a "sell by" or "best before" date, so check this and make sure that there are no signs of damage to packages, cans, or jars.

Food that is stored in the refrigerator should be in clean, covered containers. Store cooked and raw foods on separate shelves and put raw meat and fish on plates or in dishes, so their juices cannot drip onto foods on the shelf below. Check the package to see that the food is suitable for freezing, and never freeze foods for longer than the time recommended by the manufacturer. Always defrost frozen foods thoroughly before using, and never refreeze food once it has been defrosted. Defrost meats and poultry in the refrigerator, never at room temperature.

COOKING AND REHEATING

Always cook your baby's food very thoroughly, especially meat, poultry, and eggs. Never give your baby raw or soft-cooked eggs. It is best not to give your baby reheated leftovers or foods that have been refrozen. If you're preparing food in bulk quantities, don't let it cool before putting it into the refrigerator because this will give the bacteria a chance to multiply. Put the food in cold containers, cover them tightly, and put them right into the refrigerator or freezer.

PREPARING

At first, you'll have to purée all of your baby's food, but this stage won't last very long. If you don't have a blender or food processor, an inexpensive hand-operated food mill will do. A nylon strainer will be perfectly adequate to begin with. As your baby gets older, you can feed him coarser foods. By the time he is six months old, he will be able to manage a thicker purée, and at nine months he can enjoy a mixture with small chunks of meat or vegetables in it.

You can use a variety of liquids to thin home-prepared foods. The water you've used to steam fruits or vegetables is ideal because it contains valuable nutrients. To thicken foods, you can use ground, whole grain cereals such as wheatgerm, or cottage cheese, yogurt, or mashed potatoes. If you feel you need to sweeten foods, use naturally sweet fruit juice rather than refined sugar.

TIPS FOR PREPARING FOODS SAFELY

DO…	DON'T…
• Use fruits and vegetables as soon as possible after buying.	• Buy bruised or wrinkled fruits and vegetables.
• Peel tough-skinned fruits and vegetables if the skin is likely to cause your baby problems.	• Leave prepared vegetables to soak in water, since this destroys their vitamins.
• Cook soft-skinned fruits and vegetables in their skins. This helps retain their vitamins and provides additional fiber.	• Slice or cut up fruits and vegetables a long time in advance, since their vitamin content will be lost.
• Cook fruits and vegetables in a steamer, in a tightly covered pan with very little water, or microwave. This helps retain the vitamins that are normally lost in cooking.	• Give red meat more than twice a week, since it has a high saturated fat content.
• Give your baby cooked and puréed meat or fish. The purée can be thinned with vegetable water or soup.	• Overcook or boil canned foods, since this destroys their vitamins.
• Use safflower or corn oil. Never cook with butter or other saturated fats.	• Add salt or sugar to your child's food. His immature kidneys can't handle a great deal of salt, and giving him sweet foods at an early age will encourage a sweet tooth.
	• Leave prepared foods to cool at room temperature: refrigerate them right away.

PROCESSED FOODS

Processed foods are more expensive than foods you make at home, but they are convenient, especially if you are in a hurry or traveling. Always observe the following guidelines when using them.

- *Check the ingredients; they are listed in order of quantity, with the greatest amount first. Anything that has water or sugar near the top of the list will not be very nutritious.*

- *Avoid all foods with added sugar or modified starch. It is illegal for baby foods to contain added salt or monosodium glutamate (MSG).*

- *Make sure that any seal is intact. If it is damaged, the food could be contaminated.*

- *Don't heat up the food in the jar: the glass might crack.*

- *Don't feed your baby from the jar if you intend to keep some of the food, because the leftovers will be contaminated with saliva. You can feed your baby from the jar if he's likely to eat the whole amount.*

- *Don't keep opened jars in the refrigerator for longer than two days and never beyond the "best before" or "sell by" date.*

- *Never store food in an opened can. Transfer it to a dish, cover, and refrigerate.*

- *Check the ingredients lists carefully if you are introducing food types gradually. Many processed foods contain eggs, gluten, and dairy products.*

FRUITS AND VEGETABLES

Fresh fruits and vegetables are best; frozen are second best. If you use canned varieties, be sure to check the labels so you can avoid those with additives and extra salt and sugar.

Fresh vegetables are rich in nutrients, colors, flavors, and textures. Wash leafy vegetables and scrub root vegetables rather than peeling, if possible, since most nutrients lie just beneath the skin. Cook for the least amount of time as soon

FACTS ABOUT FRESH VEGETABLES AND HOW TO USE THEM

TYPE	HOW TO USE
ASPARAGUS	Good in soups, quiches, salads. Simmer for 10 minutes. Serve only the tips.
AVOCADOS	Always peel. Good texture for babies. A rich source of unsaturated fat.
BEAN SPROUTS	Easily digested and full of nutrients. Good snack food. You can sprout legumes such as alfalfa beans to make your own bean sprouts at home.
BEETS	Always peel. Good in soups, sandwiches, salads, and drinks. May turn urine red, so don't be alarmed.
BROCCOLI	Rich in vitamin C. Good in soups and quiches. Avoid any with yellow tips.
BRUSSEL SPROUTS	Choose young, small ones. Simmer lightly or steam. Can be served as a finger food with cheese sauce.
CABBAGE	Stuff the leaves or use in soups and stews. Finely grate for salads.
CARROTS	Rich in vitamin A. Sweet, colorful all-rounder. Use in drinks and for baking.
CAULIFLOWER	Use unblemished florets. Easy to digest. Good in soups, sauces, and salads.
CELERIAC	Stores well. Peel. Lemon juice stops discoloration. Good in soups and salads.
CELERY	Remove stringy parts for babies. Stuff with soft cheese or purées. Use leaves too.
CHINESE CABBAGE	Mild, slightly sweet flavor. Good stir-fried. Bok choi is closely related and can be substituted.
CORN	Cook thoroughly. Hard for babies to digest.
CUCUMBER	Always peel. Stuff with cream cheese. Grate into yogurt for a quick sauce.
EGGPLANT	Always peel. Baked and puréed, it has a good creamy texture. Especially nice when mixed with a small quantity of mayonnaise.
FAVA BEANS	Serve when young and pale green. Good in soups, casseroles, and sauces.
GARLIC	An acquired taste. Always peel. Use sparingly in cooked dishes.
GREEN BEANS	Tender dwarf beans are best. Frozen are a useful standby.

as they are prepared. Baking, braising, stir-frying, steaming, and boiling are good methods; try to use any cooking juices or water in stocks, soups, and sauces. If you wish, blanch vegetables such as cauliflower to make them softer when serving them as finger foods to children under 12 months.

Check fruits for ripeness, wash well, and ideally peel them until your child is about 18 months old (then he should get used to chewing any thin peel, since it is a good source of fiber). Remove pits or seeds until he's about two years old.

FACTS ABOUT FRESH VEGETABLES AND HOW TO USE THEM

TYPE	HOW TO USE
LEEKS	Always peel. Steam, braise, or stir-fry. Good in soups or any vegetable dish.
LETTUCE	Many colorful varieties. Shred or use leaf as a container for other foods.
MUSHROOMS	Peel. Cook larger ones. Stuff with rice or cheese. Use small ones in salads.
OLIVES	Rather salty, but many children love them. Green are milder than black.
ONIONS	Always peel. Mince and use sparingly. Try milder varieties such as red onions.
PARSLEY	Rich in vitamins, iron, and minerals. Good as a garnish and in sauces.
PARSNIPS	Sweet flavor. Peel. Mash with carrots or potatoes. Purée or slice with meats.
PEAS	Use small tender peas. Purée for a bright green dip. Frozen are a good standby.
PEPPERS	Steam or grill in skins and peel. Red, yellow, and orange tend to be sweeter. Green ones are rich in vitamin C.
POTATOES	Cook in skins to retain nutrients. Purée with carrots, beets, or peas.
PUMPKIN	Always peel. Bake, steam, or sauté. Purée with cheese. Also good in pies.
RUTABAGA	Always peel. Boil and mash with yogurt. Use in soups or any savory dish.
SNOW PEAS	Eat whole or stuff. Serve with lemon juice.
SPINACH	Rich in minerals. Serve tender young leaves raw. Wash well. Cooks quickly in water clinging to leaves after washing. Good mixed with soft cheese.
SQUASH	Peel. Easily puréed. Good sautéed with cheese or herbs, or stuffed and baked.
TOMATOES	Very versatile and rich in vitamin C. Good stuffed, either raw or baked.
TURNIPS	Always peel. Takes on other flavors well when cooked. Season with herbs.
WATERCRESS	Good source of vitamins and minerals. Use in soups, salads, and sandwiches.
YAMS	Peel. Also known as sweet potato. Boil or bake. Good mashed with yogurt.
ZUCCHINI	Steam and mix with pieces of tomato for a quick meal.

FACTS ABOUT FRESH FRUITS AND HOW TO USE THEM

TYPE	HOW TO USE
APPLES	Good all-rounder and as an instant snack. Purée and add to yogurt. Bake in skins, stuffed with dried fruits.
APRICOTS	Fresh or dried. Source of vitamin A. Serve fresh ones ripe, peeled, and sliced.
BANANAS	A good first fruit. Easy to mash and mix with other foods. Good with cereals.
BLACKBERRIES	Must be ripe. Cook to a purée for juice, which stains. Good with other fruits.
CHERRIES	Must be ripe. Juice stains so supervise eating.
CURRANTS	Must be ripe. Cook and purée for babies. Use sparingly: can have a sharp taste.
DATES	Fresh or dried. Remove stones and stuff with cheese.
DRIED FRUITS	Rich in minerals. Wash and soak to soften. Serve as snacks, desserts, or as sweeteners mixed with other fruits.
FIGS	Fresh or dried. Good mixed with yogurt. Chop up for snacks.
GRAPES	Choose seedless varieties. Peel if child cannot chew skin.
GRAPEFRUIT	Choose ripe ones. Remove all pith; never add sugar. Pink varieties are sweeter.
KIWI FRUITS	Rich in vitamin C and attractive in color.
LEMONS	Use juice and finely grated peel in cooking and drinks. Juice prevents other raw fruits from discoloring.
MANGOES	Sweet and juicy. A source of vitamin A. Purée with milk for fruit dessert.
MELONS	Many varieties. Ripe pieces are refreshing and have soft flesh.
ORANGES	Like all citrus fruits, a juicy source of vitamin C. Cut off all pith for babies.
PAPAYAS	Soft, juicy texture. Good for breakfast and in salads.
PEACHES/ NECTARINES	Peaches have skins with fuzzy texture; nectarines have smooth skins. Poach or serve raw if very ripe. Use halved as a container for fruit salads.
PEARS	Good raw or baked. Also good with cubes of cheese for snacks.
PINEAPPLE	Remove core and use for teething. Juicy, fibrous fruit.
PLUMS	Many varieties. Serve very ripe ones raw, or stew in a little water with orange juice instead of sugar. Purée makes a good "jam."
PRUNES	Soak to remove stones. Stew and serve with yogurt. Purée to make a "jam."
RASPBERRIES	Good cooked or raw when ripe. Use to flavor cakes and yogurt.
RHUBARB	Stew or bake with orange rind and juice or dried fruits instead of sugar.
STRAWBERRIES	Must be ripe. Introduce at around 12 months of age. Good in tarts or chopped and mixed with fromage frais.

CHAPTER 2

EVERYDAY MEALS

There is no question that a child's diet is important
because first foods and tastes – which your child will be
trying out in her everyday meals and snacks – form the
building blocks for her future diet and health.
Here, I've set out to inspire you with some wonderful
ideas based on finger foods for children aged nine months
and up. Each meal is nutritionally balanced and,
in most cases, can be adapted from the foods you choose
and prepare for the rest of the family. You may have to
make some changes in your cooking habits, but as a
result you will probably all have a healthier diet.

RECIPE HINTS AND TIPS

The recipes for the meals featured in this book are simple and flexible. The meals focus on eggs and cheese, or fish, or meat, or vegetables, and there are also ideas for healthy snacks and picnics and food for special occasions.

Ingredients Don't hesitate to use alternative ingredients that will accommodate your child's preferences, or to use a food processor or blender to speed up preparation time. Where a recipe calls for flour, oil, or sugar, try to use whole-wheat flour, polyunsaturated vegetable oils, and raw brown sugar, which has a stronger flavor than white refined sugar, so you can use less to sweeten cookies and cakes. Honey isn't used in the recipes. It is just another form of sugar, and it is wise not to give it to children under 12 months since it may contain harmful bacteria.

If you want to use salt in a dish for all the family, add it after removing your child's portion. This way, you will be encouraging a taste for real food rather than a taste for salt. Add herbs and spices for flavor instead.

Storage If a recipe makes more than you need, you can store the surplus in a covered, airtight container in the refrigerator; use within two days. Alternatively, you can freeze food, closely wrapped, for up to one month.

Stainless-steel grater

Handheld blender

Preparing first foods
While your baby is getting used to solids, you will need to grate or purée vegetables for her. Steaming is a fast cooking method that helps to preserve all the nutrients.

Grated carrot

Collapsible steamer fits any pan

BREAKFAST

CEREALS

WHITE RICE

BROWN RICE

BARLEY

COMMERCIAL BABY RICE

We should all eat more whole-grain cereals and, by including them in your child's diet from the beginning, you may come to eat more of them yourself. For most babies, their first solid food is an iron-rich commercial baby cereal. However, you can make your own mixes and grind them in a blender to get a finer texture. Use rice, oats, barley, rye, millet, and wheat. Later, add dried or fresh fruits and ground nuts, and serve the cereal mixed with milk, yogurt, or diluted apple juice. With ready-to-eat brands, read the labels carefully. Few are free of added salt and sugar, but you should be able to find unsweetened, salt-free brands if you shop around. Don't limit cereals to breakfast time. Use them as a topping, a thickener, a coating, and when you bake, and don't forget the less common varieties such as cornmeal and bulgar wheat.

BULGAR WHEAT

COMMERCIAL CEREAL

MILLET

GROUND MUESLI

CORNMEAL

SEMOLINA

ROLLED OATS

BREADS

PUMPERNICKEL
BREAD

SEVEN-
GRAIN
BREAD

FRENCH
BREAD

LIGHT RYE BREAD
WITH CARAWAY SEEDS

Whole-wheat bread is the best
to serve your child, but many other
high-fiber, whole grain breads are
available (the grains in seven-grain bread
may be too tough for young babies).
If your child eats these most of the time,
the occasional slice of white bread is fine.
Always read the label carefully when
buying packaged bread. Some brown
breads are not whole wheat at all and
contain coloring. If you bake your own
bread, try to use 100 percent whole-
wheat flour and experiment with adding
wheatgerm, sesame seeds, and bran for
extra flavor. You can make any bread
look attractive by cutting it into shapes
using small cookie cutters and serving
it with different spreads.

SODA BREAD

WHOLE-WHEAT BREAD
(recipe p. 41)

CORNBREAD
(recipe p. 41)

FRUIT BREAD

PUMPERNICKEL BREAD

TELL-THE-TIME BREAKFAST

Bread, egg, soft cheese, and fruit are formed into a clock shape to make this breakfast. Older children will enjoy eating their way around the clock as they try to tell the time, and younger ones will simply like its shape. The bread pieces are dipped in beaten egg with a spoonful of milk added to it. After soaking the bread thoroughly, fry it quickly in a nonstick skillet brushed with a little oil. For a quicker meal, simply spread pieces of whole-wheat bread with a fruity jam, fruit purée such as prune, or soft cheese and chopped fruit. Fruit is a good instant food, even at breakfast time, and you should try to serve a few slices of fresh fruit every day, as a snack and with meals.

Breakfast clock face with whole-wheat bread
Dip eight bread pieces in egg and milk and fry. Spread four pieces with ricotta cheese and diced dried apricots. Arrange in a clock face and add banana for the hands. *(Recipe p. 41)*

Slices of watermelon, seeded

Ricotta cheese mixed with diced dried apricots

Banana clock hands

French toast

SUNSHINE BREAKFAST

Every household has its own idea of what the traditional breakfast should be, but with young children, who are usually ravenous as soon as they wake up in the mornings, speed is of the essence. This cheery breakfast is a change from the usual cereal and does not take long to prepare. Adding dried fruits to the pancake gives it extra vitamins, fiber, and iron. Serve it with oat biscuits and fresh orange segments, which are juicy and full of vitamin C (you may want to cut the pieces in half for younger children). Pancakes can be made in batches and then frozen. To serve, just defrost at room temperature and toast them lightly so they heat through.

Juicy fresh orange segments
Remove all the peel, pith, and seeds so that there is no risk of choking. Arrange the segments to look like the sun's rays.

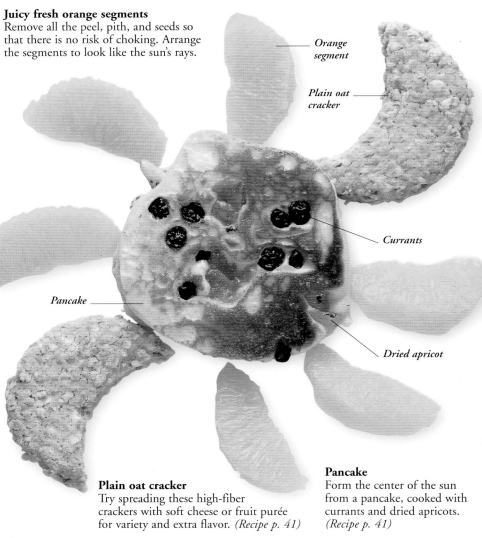

Orange segment

Plain oat cracker

Currants

Pancake

Dried apricot

Plain oat cracker
Try spreading these high-fiber crackers with soft cheese or fruit purée for variety and extra flavor. *(Recipe p. 41)*

Pancake
Form the center of the sun from a pancake, cooked with currants and dried apricots. *(Recipe p. 41)*

BREAKFAST RECIPES

CORNBREAD *(page 38)*

Ingredients for 1 large cornbread
2½ cups (275 g) self-rising flour
½ cup (100 g) sugar
2 tbsp baking powder
pinch of salt
2 cups (225 g) yellow cornmeal
4 eggs, beaten
2½ cups (600 ml) milk
¼ lb (100 g) butter or margarine, melted

1 Preheat oven to 400°F (200°C).
2 Mix all the dry ingredients together.
3 Add the lightly beaten eggs, milk, and butter and mix for 1 minute until smooth.
4 Grease a 12 x 9 in (30 x 23 cm) baking pan and pour in the mixture.
5 Bake for 35 minutes. Cut into squares and serve warm.

WHOLE-WHEAT BREAD *(page 39)*

Ingredients for 1 small loaf
3 cups (350 g) whole-wheat flour
⅔ cup (210 ml) water
½ envelope (3 g) quick-acting dry yeast
1 table spoon vegetable oil
pinch of salt

1 Preheat oven to 450°F (230°C).
2 Place all the ingredients in a mixing bowl and mix together to form a dough.
3 Turn the dough onto a board and knead vigorously for 5 minutes.
4 Place the dough in a clean mixing bowl, cover, and leave in a warm place to rise.
5 When the dough has doubled in size, form it into rolls and place on a greased baking sheet. Alternatively, form it into a loaf shape and place in a greased 8 x 4 x 2½ in (500 g) loaf pan.
6 Bake rolls for 15–20 minutes, a loaf for 25–35 minutes, or until the bread sounds hollow when tapped on the bottom.
7 Transfer rolls or turn out loaf onto a wire rack to cool thoroughly.

PANCAKES *(page 40)*

Ingredients for about 15 pancakes
1 cup (100 g) flour
1 tsp baking soda
1½ tsp cream of tartar
1 egg
⅔ cup (150 ml) milk
handful of dried fruits such as currants and apricots

1 Sift the dry ingredients into a bowl.
2 Make a well in the center, crack in the egg, and add the milk. Mix to a batter.
3 Heat a small, nonstick skillet and brush with a little oil. Drop a spoonful of the batter onto the hot surface.
4 Sprinkle dried fruit onto the batter and turn over when bubbles appear on the surface (after 1 or 2 minutes). Cook for a minute or two to brown the other side.
5 Repeat with rest of batter. Wrap the pancakes in a clean cloth to keep warm.
6 To freeze, cool and store in a container between layers of waxed paper.

PLAIN OAT CRACKERS *(page 40)*

Ingredients for about 20 crackers
½ cup (50 g) flour
1½ cups (175 g) oatmeal
½ cup (50 g) rolled oats
pinch of baking soda
¼ lb (100 g) butter or margarine
1 egg yolk

1 Preheat oven to 350°F (180°C).
2 Mix all the dry ingredients together.
3 Rub in the fat until the mixture resembles fine bread crumbs.
4 Mix to a firm dough with the egg yolk.
5 Turn onto a board and knead lightly. Roll out to a thickness of ¼ in (6 mm).
6 Cut into shapes with cookie cutters or a knife. Transfer to a greased baking sheet.
7 Bake the crackers for about 15 minutes, or until they are lightly browned.

EGG AND CHEESE MEALS

EGG SAILBOATS

Although eggs are a good source of protein and iron, you should introduce them into your child's diet gradually – first the yolk, then the white when she is 10–12 months old. Check for any reaction or allergy (see p. 27) and use sparingly. Three or four eggs a week is about right for young children, so if you use eggs a lot in cooking, offer slices rather than halves when serving these sailboats. Add a portion of whole-wheat bread and a brightly colored, tempting vegetable. Snow peas, shown here stuffed with mashed cottage cheese, are tender and fun to eat. Alternatively, fill crisp lettuce hearts or lightly steamed or raw celery sticks with the fibrous strands removed.

Gouda cheese

Bread fish
Serve whole-wheat bread cut into shapes.

Hard-boiled egg

Cottage cheese

Cooked pea

Snow pea

Green pea boat
Steam snow peas, split, and fill with mashed cottage cheese. Decorate each boat with cooked green peas.

Chewy apricot slices
Spread puréed apricots on a baking tray and bake in the oven at its lowest setting for 8 hours. Cool and store in the refrigerator.

Egg sailboats
Hard-boil an egg and cut it in half. Cut triangles from a slice of Gouda cheese for the sails. Make an incision in the egg halves to secure the sails.

Apricot slice

CAT AND MOUSE

If your child has been introduced to a cat or a story about a cat and a mouse, she will find these shapes particularly interesting. The cat's face is a simple one-egg omelet with diced boiled potato and fresh parsley added to it. Parsley is rich in calcium, iron, and vitamins. Serve it finely chopped as an edible garnish to add color to any meal. Fill the omelet with any vegetables you have on hand so that it holds its shape. Add extra flavor and texture with herbs, grated cheese, or crunchy bean sprouts. Cut the omelet into strips and reassemble the shape before adding the lettuce, carrot, and celery strip features so that your child can eat the pieces of omelet as finger food.

Raisin nose

Peeled, seedless grape halves

Cat-face omelet
Make the cat's features from lettuce leaves, pieces of cooked carrot, and steamed celery strips, and its face from a light one-egg omelet, made extra nutritious with parsley and diced vegetables. *(Recipe p. 48)*

Crisp lettuce heart ears

Strip of fresh pear

Pear mouse
Peel a ripe pear, cut it in half, and core. Peel a seedless grape, cut it in half and secure in slits for the ears. Use a strip of pear for the mouse's tail and add a raisin for its nose.

Omelet

Carrot nose and eyes

Sliced celery whiskers

43

CHEESY MONSTER

This friendly monster is easily made from a simple, tasty cheese and lentil dish, cut into shapes and decorated with a realistic spiny back, forked tail, and sturdy legs. Lentils are economical, quick to cook, and extremely nutritious, whether you choose red, brown, or green varieties. They mix well with any cooked vegetable and make a protein-rich meal when prepared in combination with cheese, egg, and whole-wheat bread crumbs or wheatgerm. The dip-style dessert is a blend of low-fat cottage cheese or ricotta and raspberry purée (you may need to strain the purée to get rid of seeds). The mixture is perfect for dipping pieces of fresh fruit, crackers, or even fingers.

Cheesy monster
The cheese and lentil dish that forms the monster can be served hot or cold. Soft steamed zucchini provides a nice contrast of texture. *(Recipe p. 48)*

Sliced green olive

Squeeze of tomato purée

Raspberry dip
Purée ripe or lightly cooked raspberries without sugar. Mix with the same amount of low-fat cottage cheese or ricotta and serve the dip with fresh fruit or biscuits.

Peeled raw apple

Cheese and lenti[l] dish forms the body and head

MAKING THE MOST OF CHEESE

Cheese in any form is an excellent food for children, but don't rely only on traditional hard, high-fat cheeses like cheddar. Try medium-fat cheeses such as Edam, Gouda, and Swiss, and Scandinavian varieties like Emmenthal or Jarlsberg. These are mild in flavor and many have holes, which children like. Don't hesitate to introduce soft French cheeses, but make sure you use only those that are prepared from pasteurized milk. Camembert and Brie are often favorites because of their creamy texture and mild flavor. Remove the rind before serving. Low-fat soft cheeses such as cottage cheese and ricotta are easy to digest and can be added to dishes in place of milk.

Soft steamed zucchini

EDAM AS A RABBIT

LOW-FAT SOFT CHEESE AS A BUTTERFLY

GRILLED BRIE AS A STAR

JARLSBERG AS A GIRAFFE

CHEESE ON TOAST AS A PENGUIN

RICOTTA AND CHOPPED APRICOTS AS A HEART

Exciting cheese shapes
Cutting hard or firm cheese into shapes with miniature cookie cutters will add to its appeal for your child.

45

SMILEY-FACE PIZZA

Pizza is a favorite meal for the whole family and can be prepared in individual portions to suit your child. You can make it with a traditional yeast dough or a scone dough, as here, which is quicker. For extra speed, use half of an English muffin or a slice of pita bread as a base. Lightly toast one side, put some grated cheese on the other, spread on the topping, decorate, and broil until the cheese melts. The basic pizza topping of tomatoes, chopped onions, and cheese can be livened up for the rest of the family with tuna, anchovies, or olives. Keep your child's portion lighter in flavor and allow it to cool before serving. Cheese retains its heat and can easily scald a youngster's mouth.

Smiley-face pizza
This all-in-one meal consists of a scone-based pizza decorated with cheese, vegetables, and pieces of fresh fruit.
(Recipe p. 48)

Alfalfa sprouts

Mozzarella cheese

Kiwi fruit

Mushroom slice

Green pepper slice

Pizza

Peeled seedless grape

Peeled kiwi fruit

QUICHE FLOWER

Most adults were brought up to believe that the savory part of any meal ought to be eaten first, but by serving savory and sweet foods together, you are offering your child a wider choice in flavors. There is no harm in starting off a meal with something sweet, such as these slices of mango or any other fresh fruit. But avoid letting your child fill up on sugary and fattening candy, cakes, cookies, and desserts. Try to liven up dishes that would otherwise look plain by adding brightly colored edible garnishes: the watercress used here is rich in vitamin A and many minerals. This wholesome meal gets an extra boost to its nutritional value in a cup of naturally sweet carrot juice.

Quiche flower
Serve fresh fruit alongside a vegetable quiche made with whole-wheat pastry for a complete meal. *(Recipe p. 48)*

Watercress to garnish

Mango slices arranged to look like petals

Quiche

Carrot juice
Make this in a food processor or juicer, with a dash of lemon to preserve color, or buy good-quality fresh juice.

Mango slice forms the stem

EGG AND CHEESE RECIPES

CAT-FACE OMELET *(page 43)*

Ingredients for 1 serving
1 egg
1 tbsp water
1 tbsp finely chopped parsley (and other
* herbs such as chives, optional)*
1 small potato, boiled, diced (and other
* vegetables such as bean sprouts, optional)*
small pat of butter
1 tbsp finely grated cheese (optional)
6 steamed celery strips
3 cooked carrot pieces
2 small lettuce leaves

1 Beat egg lightly with water, chopped parsley, and other herbs, if using. Mix in the potato and other vegetables, if using.
2 Heat butter in a small skillet until it foams and pour in the egg mixture. Cook over medium heat until lightly set, then sprinkle on the cheese, if using.
3 When the omelet is set, slide it out of the skillet and cut into slices.
4 Reassemble the omelet and decorate.

CHEESY MONSTER *(pages 44–45)*

Ingredients for about 8 pieces
1 cup (225 g) red lentils
2 cups (450 ml) water
1 onion, finely chopped
1 tbsp oil
¼ lb (100 g) cheese, grated
1 tsp chopped fresh herbs
1 egg, beaten
½ cup (25 g) whole-wheat bread crumbs
* or wheatgerm*
tomato purée and slices of green olive

1 Preheat oven to 375°F (190°C).
2 Cook the lentils in the water until soft and all the liquid has been absorbed.
3 Sauté the onion in the oil until soft.
4 Mix all the ingredients together and press into a greased 9 in (23 cm) cake pan.
5 Bake for 30 minutes. Serve hot or cold.

SMILEY-FACE PIZZA *(page 46)*

Ingredients for 1 large pizza
1 onion, chopped
1 garlic clove, crushed
1 tbsp oil
1 lb (450 g) fresh tomatoes, peeled
* and chopped*
2 tbsp tomato paste
1 tsp chopped fresh oregano or basil
4 tbsp (50 g) margarine
2 cups (225 g) self-rising flour
½ cup (50 g) grated cheese
⅔ cup (150 ml) milk
small pieces of mozzarella cheese
1 slice each of mushroom and green pepper

1 Preheat oven to 400°F (200°C).
2 Sauté the onion and garlic in the oil to soften. Add the tomatoes, tomato paste, and herbs. Cover. Simmer for 20 minutes.
3 Meanwhile, rub the fat into the flour. Add half the grated cheese and gradually mix in the milk to form a soft dough.
4 Roll out the dough into a 10 in (25 cm) circle. Place on a greased baking sheet and sprinkle with the other half of the cheese.
5 Spread the tomato topping mixture over the base and decorate as desired.
6 Bake for about 30 minutes.

QUICHE FLOWER *(page 47)*

Ingredients
precooked whole-wheat pastry shell in
* 7–8 in (18–20 cm) tart pan*
2 eggs
1¼ cups (300 ml) milk
1 cup (100 g) chopped raw vegetables such
* as leeks, tomatoes, and mushrooms*
½ cup (50 g) grated cheese

1 Preheat oven to 350°F (180°C).
2 Combine the eggs, milk, and vegetables.
3 Pour into the tart shell, sprinkle with cheese, and bake for 20 minutes, or until a knife inserted in the center comes out clean.

MEALS WITH FISH

FUNNY FISH

Fish is such a nutritious food that everybody should try to eat more on a regular basis. Prepare it in a variety of ways. Steam it, bake it with herbs and vegetables, poach it in milk, or coat it with a cereal mixture for broiling or baking. Double check that there are no bones in the fish before serving. For additional fun, arrange the fish pieces into a shape that your child will recognize. Serve them with crisp and colorful vegetables, such as the rutabaga and cherry tomato used here, and chewy foods like these little dried fruit balls. A slice of whole-wheat bread is also a good accompaniment. Make it a rule never to leave your child alone when she is eating since there is always the risk of choking. Besides, meals should be sociable times and not solitary occasions.

Dried fruit balls
These chewy little morsels are made from dried fruit, puffed rice, and peanuts.
(Recipe p. 53)

Dried fruit balls are nutritious and satisfying

Cooked rutabaga, cut into slices _____

Funny fish
Brighten up any mealtime with sunny yellow slices of rutabaga filled with poached fish and topped with a bright red tomato.
(Recipe p. 53)

_____ *Poached fish*

Cherry tomato

Emmenthal cheese, shaped like a fish

FISH STICK TREE

Fish is an excellent source of protein. It's also delicate in flavor, low in fat, and easy for young children to digest. Try to buy fresh, not frozen, fish and remove the skin and bones before serving (easier to do after cooking). The fish stick for this tree is homemade, but good commercial brands are available. Check the list of ingredients on the label and remove the coating if it has artificial coloring. You can make your own attractive and nutritious coatings with any combination of grains, cereals, seeds, or dry bread crumbs. Remember to let the broiled or baked fish cool before serving it.

Fish stick tree
Form the trunk of this sturdy tree from a homemade fish stick with a crunchy coating. Arrange bright green steamed broccoli florets around it for the branches and cherry tomatoes for the colorful flowers. *(Recipe p. 53)*

Steamed broccoli floret

Skinned cherry tomato

Fruity flower
Use a special cutter to shape the melon-ball center of this flower. Surround it with juicy segments of fresh orange and give it a melon slice for the stem.

Orange segment

Fish stick

Honeydew melon

Edam cheese for a gatepost

Italian breadstick for a fence

JUMPING SHRIMP

Shrimp are frequently great favorites with children: they're easy to hold, an appealing color, and good to chew on. However, it's best to avoid serving shellfish to children under a year, since it can cause an allergic reaction if eaten too soon. Tomatoes (like potatoes) make excellent containers. Fill them with any ingredients and serve as a dip. Since tomatoes are a rich source of vitamin C and are available fresh all year round, you should try to serve them often in a variety of ways. The fruit turnover is cut open to make a butterfly shape and show off its colorful filling.

Cooked, peeled shrimp

Cooked green pea

Butterfly turnover
Stewed pears and raspberries make a sweet, juicy filling for this whole-wheat pastry turnover. *(Recipe p. 53)*

Fresh pear for antenna

Jumping shrimp
Skin small tomatoes and scoop out the seeds. Fill with a mixture of cottage cheese, mashed potato, and peas. Arrange the shrimp so that they appear to jump out of the tomatoes.

Cottage cheese and mashed potato

Tomato

TUNA POTATO BOAT

Scrubbed potatoes, baked in their skins and stuffed with a variety of fillings, served with a few vegetables or a small salad, provide a complete, balanced meal for any member of the family. This boat is filled with scooped-out potato mixed with tunafish and yogurt (cottage cheese or ricotta would do just as well). Alternatively, make a filling using a variety of different vegetables and some grated cheese, ground meat, or flaked fish. The potato will have cooled to the right temperature for your child to eat by the time you have prepared the filling. Slices of fresh papaya work well for dessert. Try to serve some fresh fruit with every meal so that it becomes a healthy lifetime habit.

Potato boat with three funnels
Give this tunafish- and yogurt-stuffed potato boat extra appeal for your child with three funnels made of carrot, rutabaga, and celery.

Peeled, seedless grapes for puffs of smoke

Baked rutabaga funnel

Steamed carrot funnel

Steamed celery funnel

Flaked tuna with yogurt and potato

Baked potato

Peeled papaya slice

FISH RECIPES

FUNNY FISH *(page 49)*

Ingredients for 1 serving
small pat of butter
1 smoked haddock, about 6 oz (175 g)
(check that the color is not artificial)
3 tbsp milk
3 tbsp water
1 fresh or dried bay leaf
slices of peeled, cooked rutabaga
1 cherry tomato

1 Lightly butter the inside of a saucepan.
2 Place the haddock in the pan. Add the milk and water to just cover the fish and the bay leaf. Bring slowly to a boil.
3 Simmer very gently for 5–10 minutes, until the fish flakes easily with a knife.
4 Take the fish out of the pan, using a slotted spoon, remove any skin and bones, and flake into bite-size pieces.
5 Decorate with the rutabaga and tomato.

DRIED FRUIT BALLS *(page 49)*

Ingredients for about 20 balls
4 tbsp (50 g) margarine
6 oz (175 g) dried fruit such as raisins
or chopped apricots, prunes, or dates
2 eggs, beaten
1 cup (75 g) puffed rice cereal
½ cup (65 g) ground nuts

1 Melt the margarine in a large saucepan over low heat.
2 Stir in the dried fruit and beaten eggs, mix well, and heat until thickened (about 10 minutes), but do not allow the mixture to boil or the eggs will scramble.
3 Stir in the cereal and nuts. Let cool, and then shape into about 20 small balls.
4 Place the fruit balls on a baking sheet, cover, and chill until firm.
5 Store between sheets of waxed paper in an airtight container in the refrigerator.
Note: not suitable for children under a year or who are allergic to eggs.

FISH STICK TREE *(page 50)*

Ingredients for about 16 fish sticks
1 lb (450 g) white fish fillets
¾ cup (75 g) yellow cornmeal
3 tbsp (35 g) sesame seeds
1 tsp paprika
2 eggs, beaten
2 tbsp safflower oil
steamed broccoli and cherry tomatoes

1 Preheat oven to 350°F (180°C).
2 Cut the fish fillets into 1 x 4 in (3 x 10 cm) pieces.
3 Mix the cornmeal, seeds, and paprika.
4 Whisk the eggs and oil together.
5 Roll each fish piece in the cornmeal mixture, then soak in the egg mixture. Roll again in the cornmeal to coat well.
6 Place on a greased baking sheet and bake in the oven for 10 minutes, turning the fish after 5 minutes to cook evenly.
7 Decorate with broccoli and tomatoes.

BUTTERFLY TURNOVER *(page 51)*

Ingredients for 2 turnovers
6 tbsp (75 g) margarine or butter
1⅔ cups (175 g) whole-wheat flour
1½ tbsp water
¼ cup (50 g) diced stewed pears
¼ cup (25 g) fresh raspberries
a little beaten egg

1 Preheat oven to 400°F (200°C).
2 Rub the fat into the flour until the mixture resembles fine bread crumbs.
3 Add the water a little at a time so the mixture binds together but is not sticky.
4 Roll out the pastry on a floured board to a thickness of about ⅛ in (3 mm). Cut into oval shapes with a pastry cutter.
5 Mix the pear and raspberries and divide among the shapes. Brush the edges with beaten egg, fold over, and seal.
6 Place the turnovers on a greased baking sheet and bake for 15–20 minutes.

MEALS WITH MEAT

CRAB TURNOVER

Although it is best to use whole-wheat pastry most of the time, puff pastry can make a light and airy change. This appetizing turnover is filled with a mixture of cooked chicken, spinach, and tiny cauliflower florets, but any combination of vegetables, meat, fish, or cheese will do. Test that the center is completely cooled before serving it to your child. Cut crosswise into pieces to make it finger food. Pastry is an excellent standby for savory or dessert dishes and is a useful item to have in the freezer. Prepare it in small batches to freeze or alternatively buy an additive-free commercial brand. Use the pastry to make open tarts, filled pies, turnovers, and any variety of shaped bases.

Whole-wheat pastry

Crab turnover with meat and vegetables
Thinly roll out ready-made puff pastry, fill with any cooked meat and vegetables, and bake in a hot oven until golden. Add claws of whole-wheat pastry and Edam cheese to make the turnover into a crab.

Orange starfish
Remove all the pith and seeds from fresh orange segments and arrange them to look like a starfish.

Chicken, spinach, and cauliflower filling

Edam cheese for claws

Soft cheese shell
Shape a spoonful of ricotta into a shell by using a tiny mold lined with plastic wrap. This makes it easier to turn out the cheese.

CHICKEN CHEWS

The first meat a child tries is often chicken, and it frequently remains a favorite. Served as it is here, it becomes a meal that the whole family will enjoy. Simply cut your child's portion into bite-size, easy-to-handle pieces and arrange them in a funny shape. Choose skinned and boned chicken breast. It is always important to remove the skin because most of the fat lies right beneath it, which makes it unhealthy to eat. Coat the poultry in beaten egg and a ground cereal mixture, bread crumbs, or cornmeal before baking and serve a green vegetable with it. Assorted chopped fresh fruit, served in half an orange with the flesh scooped out, makes a tempting and pretty dessert.

Chicken chews
Arrange crunchy-coated chicken pieces with green beans and sautéed potatoes to make this amusing caterpillar. *(Recipe p. 62)*

Orange basket of fresh fruits
Fill an orange shell with peeled and seedless orange segments, strawberries, and peeled, seedless green grapes.

Grape

Orange

Strawberry

Chicken coated with cornmeal

Sautéed potato

Steamed green bean

TASTY TEDDY BEAR

The teddy bear is a beloved toy of most children, and one they will recognize from an early age. This is an ideal meal to prepare whenever you've cooked turkey or chicken for your family and pieces are left over. Don't be tempted to use cooked meat that is more than 24 hours old: it may contain harmful bacteria that will make your child sick. The teddy bear is made from a chopped turkey and mashed potato mixture that is coated with oatmeal and baked in the oven. You can easily adapt the recipe to use any ingredients you have on hand such as flaked fish, mashed cooked legumes, or ground lean meat. Serve with a steamed fresh vegetable and slices of fresh fruit.

Citrus fruits are rich in vitamin C

Tasty teddy bear
A favorite toy becomes an edible mealtime treat when made with turkey or chicken croquettes for its head and body and steamed carrots for its ears, eyes, nose, limbs, and buttons. *(Recipe p. 62)*

Grapefruit segment without pith and seeds

Peeled mango slice

Peeled carrot, steamed until soft, for limbs, features, ears, and buttons

Turkey or chicken croquette

MERRY MEATBALL PONY

Small meatballs are a perfect finger food and simple to prepare, particularly if you are making them for the rest of the family. Use top-quality ground lean beef or lamb. It is worth the cost for the flavor and lack of fat. You can bind the meatballs with egg and other ingredients such as rolled oats, wheatgerm, or whole-wheat bread crumbs and flavor them with grated cheese or herbs of your choice. Broil or bake the meatballs to give them a crunchy coating. Steam or stir-fry the accompanying vegetables so that they keep valuable nutrients, crispness, and color. To add interest to the dessert, top a slightly sweetened oatmeal cookie with fruit and ricotta or plain yogurt.

Merry meatball pony
Arrange three crunchy coated mini-meatballs with steamed or stir-fried carrots to produce this friendly creature. Alfalfa sprouts on the side add extra interest. *(Recipe p. 62)*

Oatmeal cookie dessert
A homemade cookie becomes a healthy dessert when topped with slices of peeled plum and ricotta cheese or plain yogurt. *(Recipe p. 62)*

Oatmeal cookie

Steamed carrot triangles for ears

Plain yogurt

Meatballs for the body and head

Peeled ripe yellow plum

Steamed carrot strips for legs

Alfalfa sprouts for grass

MEATLOAF CAR

A slice of meatloaf is almost a complete meal in itself with its blend of meat, vegetables, and bread crumbs. Whenever you make meatloaf for the family, you can cut off a piece for your child and shape it quickly and easily, or use cookie cutters for fancy shapes. Add a few vegetables for extra color and flavor. You can even arrange vegetables in the loaf to make patterns by packing the meat mixture into the baking dish with alternating layers of carrot rings, green peas, or sliced mushrooms. If you don't have any meatloaf, simply make this car shape from a slice of whole-wheat bread spread with chicken salad and decorated with strips of cucumber or green beans. For a treat, bake a delicious whole-wheat sponge cake with a layer of sliced fruit on the bottom for extra moisture and interest. Cut it into small pieces for serving.

Meatloaf car
Form a sturdy car from slices of meatloaf, then add steamed zucchini for the wheels. Arrange chicory leaves to make the road.
(Recipe p. 62)

Whole-wheat cake
Put small pieces of whole-wheat sponge cake under the car to represent a bridge. Bite-size chunks of fruit in the cake are a succulent surprise.
(Recipe p. 63)

Meatloaf

Steamed zucchini

Chicory leaf

Pineapple

Glacé cherry

Cake

RATTLE MUNCH

This extra-nutritious beef burger is a tasty mixture of lean ground meat, bulgar wheat, grated cheese, or shredded vegetables such as zucchini for moisture, and mixed herbs for flavor. Give the burger added texture and fiber with a coating of cooked brown rice, barley, rolled oats, wheatgerm, or sesame seeds before baking or broiling it.

Copying the shape of your child's best-liked rattle or toy will make the meal even more tempting. Since most children enjoy meat presented like this, serve it with vegetables that are eye-catching so that they don't get overlooked in favor of the beef burger. A yogurt and fruit purée mousse provides a soft texture after the chewier main course.

Fruit mousse
For an attractive presentation, set single servings of yogurt and raspberry purée mousse in tiny molds. *(Recipe p. 63)*

Rattle munch
Recreate a toy with a cereal-coated beef burger, cherry tomatoes, unstuffed pitted green olives, and sweet potato. *(Recipe p. 63)*

Unstuffed pitted green olive

Beef burger

Cooked brown rice

Boiled and peeled sweet potato

Skinned cherry tomato

Grape juice drink
Dilute unsweetened red grape juice with water to make a delicious drink.

PIONEER LOG CABIN

Since liver is a rich source of iron, try to serve it to your child regularly. For flavor and tenderness, use calves' or lamb's liver; about 2 oz (50 g), thinly sliced, should be enough. Broil or quick-fry it so it is brown on the outside and just done but not pink inside. Avoid overcooking the liver or it will be dry, tough, and unappetizing. (You can substitute pork or chicken for the liver.)

Serve with a sauce, such as fresh tomato, to add moistness. To save time, strain a halved tomato over the liver (or meat) to remove the skin and seeds. Both the tomato and the kiwi fruit for dessert are good sources of vitamin C. Try to serve iron-rich foods, particularly grains and legumes, with those that are rich in vitamin C because this helps the body absorb iron more efficiently.

Tube-shaped pasta with strained tomato

Liver with puréed tomato

Pioneer log cabin with green beans
Make the roof from tender liver, pork, or chicken with puréed tomato. Add green beans for the walls, Edam cheese for the windows, and tubes of cooked pasta for the chimney and door frame.

Granola bar tree
Arrange a wedge of granola bar with halved pieces of kiwi fruit to form a tree. *(Recipe p. 63)*

Peeled kiwi fruit

Edam cheese

Steamed green bean

Granola bar

PICK-UP PASTA BOAT

Pasta is a great finger food. It is easy to pick up and available in many interesting shapes and colors. The shells that are used for this boat get their green color from spinach, but you could choose a pale orange variety (made with tomato) or whole-wheat pasta instead. Serve it hot or cold with any kind of sauce. This simple bolognese mixture is prepared from lean ground beef, tomatoes,

and finely chopped onion, celery, and carrot. If you wish, add fresh or dried herbs for extra flavor. Equally good sauces can be made from red, green, or brown lentils, ground skinless chicken or turkey, cheese, and virtually any finely chopped or puréed vegetable. Triangles of cheese for sails and chunks of fresh pineapple arranged as a sun complete this nautical scene.

Pick-up pasta boat
Tempt your child to eat this traditional meal of pasta with bolognese sauce by arranging it as a sailboat. The pasta and triangles of Gouda cheese can be eaten as a finger food or used to scoop up the bolognese sauce.
(Recipe p. 63)

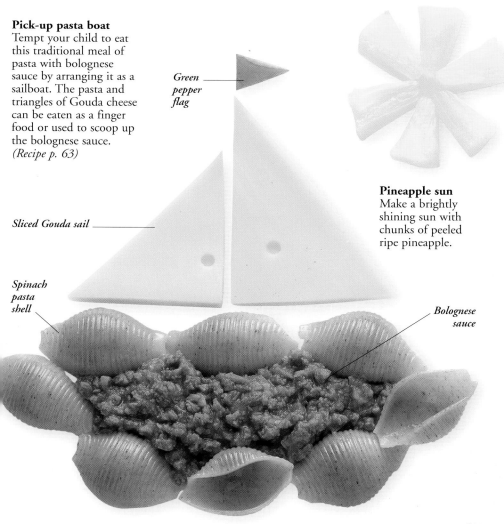

Green pepper flag

Sliced Gouda sail

Spinach pasta shell

Pineapple sun
Make a brightly shining sun with chunks of peeled ripe pineapple.

Bolognese sauce

MEAT RECIPES

CHICKEN CHEWS *(page 55)*

Ingredients for about 16 chews
1 lb (450 g) boneless chicken breast
¾ cup (75 g) cornmeal
3 tbsp (35 g) sesame seeds
1 tsp paprika
2 eggs, beaten
2 tbsp safflower oil

1 Preheat oven to 350°F (180°C).
2 Cut the chicken into bite-size cubes.
3 Coat and bake as described in the recipe
for Fish Stick Tree *(see p. 53)*.

TASTY TEDDY BEAR *(page 56)*

Ingredients for about 8 pieces
2 tbsp chopped onion
2 tbsp chopped celery
3 tbsp chopped parsley
¼ lb (100 g) potato, cooked and mashed
*   with ⅔ cup (150 ml) milk*
2 cups (350 g) minced cooked turkey
*   (or chicken)*
¼ cup (25 g) flour
1 egg, beaten with 1 tbsp milk
¾ cup (75 g) oatmeal (or other cereal)

1 Preheat oven to 350°F (180°C).
2 Mix together the first 5 ingredients and
chill until ready to use.
3 Divide into eighths and shape as desired.
4 Dip each portion into the flour and then
the egg before coating in the cereal.
5 Bake for about 10 minutes, turning over
after 5 minutes to ensure even browning.

MERRY MEATBALL PONY *(page 57)*

Ingredients for 20–30 meatballs
1 lb (450 g) lean ground beef
½ cup (50 g) rolled oats
1 small onion, finely chopped
1 egg, beaten
½ cup (50 g) grated cheese
1 tsp chopped parsley or oregano

1 Preheat oven to 350°F (180°C).
2 Mix all the ingredients together.
3 With wet hands, shape the mixture into
balls about 1 in (2.5 cm) in diameter.
4 Place on a lightly greased baking sheet
and cook, uncovered, until lightly
browned, about 20 minutes. Turn after
10 minutes to ensure even browning.

OATMEAL COOKIE *(page 57)*

Ingredients for 15–20 cookies
1½ cups (175 g) flour
¼ cup (35 g) coarse oatmeal
1 tsp baking powder
6 tbsp (75 g) butter or margarine
¼ cup (50 g) sugar
3 tbsp milk

1 Preheat oven to 350°F (180°C).
2 Mix the first 3 ingredients together.
3 Rub in the fat until the mixture
resembles fine bread crumbs.
4 Stir in the sugar and add the milk.
5 Thinly roll out and cut into shapes.
6 Place on a lightly greased baking sheet
and bake for 20 minutes.

MEATLOAF CAR *(page 58)*

Ingredients for 1 small meatloaf
½ lb (225 g) lean ground beef
1 onion, finely chopped
2 celery stalks, chopped
2 carrots, grated
1 garlic clove, crushed
1 egg, beaten
1 tsp ground cumin
2 tbsp chopped fresh parsley
1 tbsp grated Parmesan cheese
1 tbsp whole-wheat bread crumbs or
*   wheat germ*

1 Preheat oven to 350°F (180°C).
2 Mix all the ingredients thoroughly
together, then pack into a small loaf pan.
3 Bake for about 1 hour.

Whole-wheat Sponge *(page 58)*

Ingredients
¼ lb (100 g) soft margarine
½ cup (100 g) sugar
2 eggs, beaten
1 cup (100 g) whole-wheat flour, sifted
*   with 1½ tsp baking powder*
2 oz (50 g) glacé cherries, halved
2 oz (50 g) pineapple chunks

1 Preheat oven to 350°F (180°C).
2 Line one 8 in (20 cm) loaf pan with waxed paper.
3 Cream the fat and sugar together until smooth and light.
4 Gradually mix in the eggs and flour, keeping the mixture smooth.
5 Spread the fruit over the base of the pan. Spoon the mixture over the fruit and spread level. Bake for 15–20 minutes until firm. Turn out onto a wire tray. Let cool.

Rattle Munch *(page 59)*

Ingredients for about 8 pieces
1 lb (450 g) lean ground beef
2 oz (50 g) bulgar wheat
1 small onion, finely chopped
1 egg, beaten
1½ cups (50 g) grated cheese (or shredded
*   moist vegetable such as zucchini)*
1 tsp chopped mixed herbs
4 oz (100 g) cooked brown rice

1 Preheat oven to 350°F (180°C).
2 Mix all the ingredients except the rice.
3 Shape into flat rounds.
4 Roll each round in the cooked rice.
5 Place on a lightly greased baking sheet, cover with foil, and bake for 20 minutes. Remove the foil for the last 5 minutes.

Fruit Mousse *(page 59)*

Ingredients
1 envelope unflavored gelatin or vegetarian
*   substitute such as agar-agar*
2 fl oz (50 ml) cold water
4 fl oz (100 ml) boiling water
1 cup (225 ml) unsweetened fruit juice
8 oz (225 g) puréed fruit
5 fl oz (150 ml) plain yogurt

1 Pour cold water into a bowl. Sprinkle on the gelatin. Leave to soak for 1 minute.
2 Add the boiling water to the bowl and stir to dissolve the gelatin.
3 Mix in the fruit juice, fruit, and yogurt.
4 Pour into molds and chill until firm.

Granola Bar *(page 60)*

Ingredients for 15–20 pieces
1½ cups (225 g) rolled oats or muesli
⅜ cup (75 g) sugar
1 tsp baking powder
12 tbsp (150 g) butter, melted
4 oz (100 g) dried fruit and orange peel

1 Preheat oven to 300°F (150°C).
2 Mix the cereal, sugar, and baking powder together.
3 Add the melted butter and dried fruit and peel, and mix well together.
4 Pat the mixture into an ungreased 8 x 12 in (20 x 30 cm) baking sheet. Bake for about 20 minutes until golden brown. Cut into squares and allow to cool.

Pick-up Pasta Boat *(page 61)*

Ingredients for bolognese sauce
1 tsp oil
1 small onion, finely chopped
1 celery stalk, finely chopped
1 small carrot, finely chopped
1 lb (450 g) lean ground beef
1 tbsp (15 ml) tomato purée
½ cup (150 ml) beef or vegetable stock
15 oz (420 g) can chopped tomatoes

1 Heat the oil and fry the onion, celery, and carrot until softened and golden.
2 Add the ground beef and cook until browned. Add the tomato purée and cook for 1 minute.
3 Pour in the stock and tomatoes, mix well, and bring to a boil.
4 Simmer over a low heat for 45 minutes.

VEGETABLE MEALS

TRAFFIC LIGHTS

Preparing this meal does not have to be time-consuming if you have some vegetable purées in the freezer and a good assortment of pasta shapes. You can arrange purées and thick sauces in perfect circles by shaping them in a plain round pastry cutter. The jelly car is made from a simple recipe and shaped with a small cookie cutter. This kind of meal will appeal to your child by making food interesting and enjoyable to eat.

Pasta and vegetables
Arrange spinach and plain and whole-wheat pasta shapes on either side of traffic lights made from puréed tomato, carrot, and spinach. *(Recipe p. 72)*

Baked tomato purée

Cooked carrot purée

Lasagne strip

Spinach pasta shell

Spinach and potato purée

Fruit jelly car
Add texture and interest to unsweetened grape jelly with peeled fresh apple pieces and halved green grapes. *(Recipe p. 72)*

Apple

Milk drink
Think of milk as a meal in itself and serve as a snack on its own or with light meals.

Grape

BIRD'S NEST FEAST

A colorful arrangement and a variety of textures make this meal attractive, and it has lots of things to pick up and eat as finger foods. The fruity bird is sitting on a nest that contains falafel, a tasty Middle-Eastern dish made of cooked chickpeas mashed, flavored, mixed with soft bread crumbs or other cereal, and rolled into balls. For extra crunch, coat them with wheatgerm before baking. They are delicious served with a sauce of yogurt and chopped fresh mint, or yogurt and tahini (sesame paste). The salad nest is made of thin strips of whole-wheat pita bread, raw red cabbage, and lettuce, but any bread strips and shredded raw or cooked vegetables would do.

Fruity bird with tail
Golden raisins decorate a halved peach for the bird's head and body and the chunks of fresh pineapple make the tail.

Falafel ball eggs in a leafy nest
Sit the bird in a nest of lettuce, red cabbage, and pita bread, on bite-size eggs made of chickpea falafel balls. *(Recipe p. 72)*

Fresh pineapple

Golden raisins

Fresh peach, peeled and pitted

Shredded lettuce

Falafel balls

Pita bread strips

Shredded red cabbage

65

BEANY RING

Cooked beans mix well with all kinds of meat or vegetable stews and casseroles. To save time, you can use drained, canned beans or baked beans (check the label for added sugar and salt). Heat with small pieces of assorted cooked vegetables and serve in a ring of mashed potatoes, pasta, or cooked grains. Here, cooked brown rice was mixed with adzuki beans and pressed into a ring mold. Shape with a cup or a shallow glass if you don't have a mold.

Beany ring with mixed vegetables

This wholesome flower has a center of red kidney beans, celery, and cauliflower florets cooked in a tomato sauce, ringed by adzuki beans with brown rice and celery.

Red kidney bean

Celery

Tomato sauce

Cauliflower floret

Steamed celery

Brown rice mixed with adzuki beans

Strawberry milkshake
Milk blended with crushed strawberries is always a favorite summer drink.

Cooking dried legumes
These edible seeds of pod vegetables are cheap, rich in protein, iron, and minerals, and low in fats. Most need presoaking for 8–12 hours (lentils are the exception).

Red kidney beans need fast boiling for at least 10 minutes to destroy their toxins.

Black-eyed beans absorb flavors well.

Chickpeas must be cooked until soft.

Pinto beans turn pale pink when cooked.

Flageolet beans taste good and look pretty.

Cannellini beans are delicious served in tomato sauce.

Soybeans must be boiled fast for the first hour of cooking.

Adzuki beans are good mixed with rice.

Split peas are perfect for soups and purées.

Haricot beans are the original baked beans.

Lentils (either whole or split) do not need soaking and are easy for children to digest.

Lima beans have a mild taste. They keep their shape well and are ideal to serve as a finger food.

POLKA-DOT OCTOPUS

This salad is a fun and appealing way to serve beans, but do take care when first introducing them to your child. Cook the beans very thoroughly and serve in small portions until your child's sensitive digestive system is accustomed to them. Once you are familiar with the many kinds, try to use beans frequently in salads, soups, casseroles, fillings, and purées. They are colorful, rich in protein, and they pick up the flavors of other foods well. This bean salad, served in a roll, includes diced raw vegetables that you can vary according to what you have available. Whenever possible, cook different kinds of beans together to get a variety of flavors, textures, and colors in one dish.

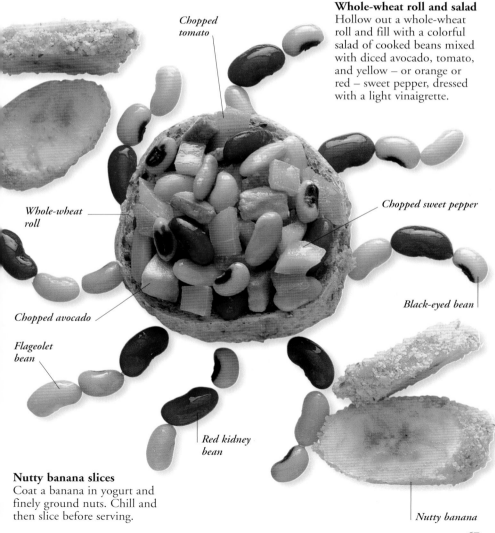

Chopped tomato

Whole-wheat roll and salad
Hollow out a whole-wheat roll and fill with a colorful salad of cooked beans mixed with diced avocado, tomato, and yellow – or orange or red – sweet pepper, dressed with a light vinaigrette.

Whole-wheat roll

Chopped sweet pepper

Black-eyed bean

Chopped avocado

Flageolet bean

Red kidney bean

Nutty banana slices
Coat a banana in yogurt and finely ground nuts. Chill and then slice before serving.

Nutty banana

LEAFY PACKAGE TRAIN

You can involve older children in preparing these vegetable packages. Younger ones will be intrigued simply by the idea of wrapping something up and unwrapping it again. Here, cabbage leaves are used as the wrapping: an outer leaf, an inner leaf, and a leaf of red cabbage. Spinach leaves would do just as well. You can fill them with any finely diced vegetables mixed with cooked grains and cheese (mushrooms, leeks, celery, barley, and cottage cheese are used here). The packages are then oven baked in stock reserved from cooking the grains. Fresh apple rings, celery, and steamed carrots add texture and complete the picture of an old-fashioned steam locomotive.

Apple-ring steam clouds
Use fancy biscuit cutters to shape peeled and cored fresh apple rings into clouds of steam.

Leafy package train
For even more realism, give the train's engine a funnel of raw celery, and position five carrot slices as wheels under the engine. (*Recipe p. 72*)

Outer cabbage leaf

Inner cabbage leaf

Raw celery

Red cabbage leaf

Steamed carrot slice

VEGETABLE ROCKET

Zucchini, tomatoes, and peppers are ideal for stuffing. Although a vegetarian mixture is used here, you could include any leftover ground lean meat or skinless chicken in the basic rice filling. If you are not preparing this dish for the rest of the family, you can speed up the cooking process by slicing the zucchini in half lengthwise, steaming it, and then mixing the pulp with the chosen filling, adding a little tahini (sesame paste) or yogurt to bind the mixture. The meal is made more substantial with a slice of whole-wheat bread spread with low-fat cheese, a pear slice cut to resemble a moon, and a tart for dessert containing slices of fresh and dried fruits to dip into its yogurt filling.

Pear moon
Let the rocket blast off toward a crescent moon made from a shaped slice of peeled ripe pear.

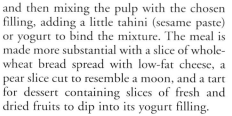

Fresh pear _____

Whole-wheat bread star
Shape the star with a cookie cutter and spread it with a low-fat cheese such as ricotta or cottage cheese.

Vegetable rocket
Stuff a zucchini half with a mixture of its own pulp, rice, onion, red pepper, and tahini (sesame paste) or yogurt. *(Recipe p. 73)*

Steamed _____
zucchini

Mixed fruit tart with yogurt
Fill a whole-wheat pastry shell with natural yogurt and sweet fresh and dried fruits for a filling dessert. *(Recipe p. 73)*

Yogurt _____

Fig _____

Prune _____

Fresh pear _____

Dried apricot

69

STIR-FRIED KITE

Stir-frying is the healthy Chinese method of cooking foods very quickly in very little oil so that they retain all their goodness. A wok is the traditional vessel for stir-frying, but you can use a small skillet over high heat. Use just a little polyunsaturated vegetable oil and whatever fresh vegetables you have available. Any combination will make a tasty dish for your child. Cubes of firm tofu are added to the stir-fry shown here. It is an ideal food for young children (and for all the family too) since it is soft, mild in flavor, easy to digest, and rich in protein and calcium. Whole-wheat pita bread, cut to look like a kite, and banana balance the meal perfectly.

Stir-fried kite with tofu
This all-in-one meal of stir-fried red and yellow sweet peppers, zucchini strips, bean sprouts, and Chinese cabbage is given extra nutritional value with cubes of firm tofu, whole-wheat pita bread, and chunks of ripe banana.

Bean sprouts

Ripe banana chunk

Whole-wheat pita bread

Zucchini strip

Firm tofu cube

Chinese cabbage

Yellow sweet pepper strand

SAVORY CONE

A leftover piece of whole-wheat pastry dough, shaped and baked quickly in a hot oven, provides the base for this cone. The topping is made of any grated vegetables, but includes cooked beets to give it a vibrant color. It is bound with a blend of plain yogurt, mayonnaise, and ground almonds. Cottage cheese or ricotta would be a quick alternative if time is short. The decoratively shaped pieces of fresh fruit and cheese are cut out with miniature cookie cutters. These finger foods let children choose which item to eat first at their own pace and help in the development of hand-to-mouth coordination. They can also be used as dippers in the soft topping.

Savory cone with soft topping
For this fun presentation, spoon a blend of grated cooked beets, ground almonds, yogurt, and mayonnaise on top of a piece of whole-wheat pastry. *(Recipe p. 73)*

Apple

_____ Apple

Gouda cheese

Mango _____

Melon _____

_____ Melon

Mango _____

Whole-wheat pastry

_____ Gouda cheese

Kiwi fruit _____

VEGETABLE RECIPES

TRAFFIC LIGHTS *(page 64)*

Ingredients
2 medium tomatoes
1 large carrot
¼ lb (100 g) spinach, well washed
1 small potato
⅔ cup (150 ml) milk
small pat of butter (optional)

1 Preheat oven to 350°F (180°C).
2 Cut a cross in the tops of the tomatoes. Place on a lightly greased baking sheet and bake for 25 minutes.
3 Steam the carrot and spinach until soft.
4 Boil the potato until soft.
5 Strain the tomatoes to remove skin and seeds, or purée and then strain.
6 Purée the carrot with the milk. Mix in the butter, if using.
7 Purée the spinach with the potato.

FRUIT JELLY CAR *(page 64)*

Ingredients
¼ cup (50 ml) cold water
1 envelope unflavored gelatin or vegetarian substitute such as agar-agar
½ cup (100 ml) boiling water
1 cup (225 ml) unsweetened fruit juice
½ lb (225 g) apples, peeled and chopped (or other fresh fruit)
handful of green grapes, halved

1 Pour cold water into a bowl. Sprinkle on the gelatin and soak for 1 minute.
2 Add the boiling water to the bowl and stir to dissolve the gelatin.
3 Mix in the fruit juice.
4 Arrange the fruit in molds or on a tray. Carefully pour over enough jelly to cover the fruit. Chill until set.
5 Pour over the rest of the jelly (slightly warm it to liquefy again, if necessary). Chill until set firm.
6 Shape the fruit jelly with a car-shaped cookie cutter if not set in molds.

FALAFEL BALL EGGS *(page 65)*

Ingredients for about 20 pieces
1 cup (275 g) chickpeas, presoaked
1 onion, finely chopped
1 garlic clove, crushed
3 tbsp (45 ml) tahini (sesame paste)
1 tsp ground cumin
2 cups (100 g) bread crumbs (or wheatgerm or rolled oats)
1 egg, beaten

1 Boil the chickpeas in fresh water until soft (between 1 and 1½ hours) or cook in a pressure cooker for 30 minutes.
2 Preheat oven to 350°F (180°C).
3 Drain the chickpeas and mash with the onion and garlic to form a thick pulp.
4 Add the tahini, cumin, bread crumbs, and beaten egg and mix well.
5 Roll the mixture into small balls. Place on a greased baking sheet and bake for 15–20 minutes.

LEAFY PACKAGE TRAIN *(page 68)*

Ingredients for 8 packages
1 cup (100 g) barley
2 leeks, chopped
2 celery stalks, chopped
8 cabbage leaves
¼ lb (100 g) mushrooms, chopped
¼ cup (50 g) soft cheese such as cottage cheese or ricotta, or grated hard cheese
1 tsp chopped mixed herbs
1 egg, beaten, to bind if necessary

1 Cover the barley with boiling water and cook for about 40 minutes, until soft. Drain, reserving the liquid, and set aside.
2 Preheat oven to 350°F (180°C).
3 Steam the leeks and celery to soften.
4 Cook the cabbage leaves in boiling water for 2 minutes, then drain and pat dry.
5 Mix together the cooked barley, all of the vegetables, the cheese, and herbs. If the mixture is too crumbly, bind with the egg.

6 Place about 1 tbsp of the filling on a cabbage leaf, fold the sides into the center, and roll up into a package. Repeat with the other cabbage leaves.
7 Place the packages, seam sides down, in a lightly greased baking dish. Add enough of the reserved barley stock to come halfway up the packages. Cover with foil and bake for about 30 minutes.

VEGETABLE ROCKET *(page 69)*

Ingredients for 8 servings
4 zucchini
2 tbsp oil
1 onion, finely chopped
1 garlic clove, crushed
1 red pepper, seeded and finely chopped
½ cup (100 g) cooked brown rice
1 tbsp tahini (sesame paste), plain yogurt, or smooth peanut butter
1¼ cups (300 ml) stock or boiling water

1 Preheat oven to 350°F (180°C).
2 Blanch the zucchini for 3–4 minutes in boiling water.
3 Cut the zucchini in half lengthwise, scoop out the centers (being careful not to pierce the shell), and chop the pulp.
4 Heat the oil in a small pan. Sauté the onion, garlic, red pepper, and zucchini pulp for 5 minutes. Mix in the rice, then add the tahini, yogurt, or peanut butter to bind the mixture.
5 Arrange the zucchini shells in a lightly greased baking dish. Divide the filling evenly among the shells and pour the stock or boiling water around them.
6 Cover with foil and bake the filled zucchini shells for 20 minutes, until the vegetables are tender.

MIXED FRUIT TART *(page 69)*

Ingredients for about 8 servings
6 tbsp (75 g) margarine or butter
1½ cups (175 g) whole-wheat flour
1½ tbsp water
1 cup (225 ml) plain yogurt
1 cup (175 g) soaked dried fruits such as figs, prunes, and apricots, cut into pieces
2 oz (50 g) fresh fruit such as pears, peeled and sliced

1 Preheat oven to 400°F (200°C).
2 Rub the fat into the flour until the mixture resembles fine bread crumbs.
3 Add the water a little at a time until the mixture binds together. The dough should be soft but not sticky.
4 Roll out the dough on a floured surface until about ⅛ in (3 mm) thick. Cut out circles with a large cookie cutter (or use a saucer as a guide) and use to line lightly greased individual tart pans.
5 To bake blind, prick the bases with a fork, cover with foil, and sprinkle with dried beans. Bake for 15 minutes, then remove the beans and foil and bake for another 5 minutes, until brown. Cool.
6 Divide the yogurt among the cooled pastry shells and arrange the fruit on top.

SAVORY CONE *(page 71)*

Ingredients for 1 serving
scraps of leftover whole-wheat pastry dough from the recipe above
1 tbsp grated cooked beets
1 tbsp cooked puréed vegetables such as carrot, rutabaga, or sweet potato
1 tbsp ground almonds
2 tsp plain yogurt
1 tsp mayonnaise

1 Preheat oven to 400°F (200°C).
2 Roll out the pastry, cut to shape, and place on a greased baking sheet. Bake for 15 minutes, until lightly browned. Cool.
3 Mix all the topping ingredients. Arrange with the pastry to form an ice-cream cone.

NUTRITIOUS SOUPS

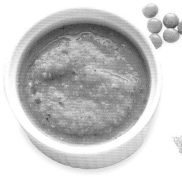

FRESH PEA SOUP
(recipe p. 75)

BORSCHT
(recipe p. 75)

SPINACH SOUP
(recipe p. 75)

Thick and hearty soups are one of the best meals you can give your child. They are also quick and easy to prepare. For a soup made in five minutes, purée any vegetables in a blender and then thin the mixture with water, milk, or yogurt. Serve hot or cold with homemade hard biscuits (see p. 76), if desired. For a thick soup, process cooked legumes or potatoes with vegetables and liquid. Keep a supply of homemade stock in the freezer and use with any vegetables you have on hand. Small children tend to like their soups rather thick for easier eating.

LENTIL SOUP
(recipe p. 76)

LIMA BEAN SOUP
(recipe p. 75)

CARROT SOUP
(recipe p. 76)

CHICKEN STOCK SOUP
(recipe p. 76)

FRESH TOMATO SOUP
(recipe p. 75)

SOUP RECIPES

FRESH PEA SOUP *(page 74)*

Makes about 6 cups (1½ liters)
1 lb (450 g) fresh peas, shelled
1 onion, chopped
1 small lettuce, roughly chopped
4½ cups (1 liter) water or stock
⅔ cup (150 ml) plain yogurt

1 Simmer the shelled peas, onion, and lettuce in the water or stock until the peas are soft, 20–30 minutes.
2 Process the mixture until smooth.
3 Add the yogurt to a little of the soup, then combine this mixture with the rest of the soup. Reheat gently, but do not allow to boil or the soup may curdle.

BORSCHT *(page 74)*

Makes about 3¾ cups (900 ml)
4 medium cooked beets, peeled
2½ cups (600 ml) milk
1 tbsp lemon juice
2 tbsp plain yogurt

1 Purée the cooked beets and combine with the milk.
2 Bring the mixture gently to a boil.
3 Remove from the heat and stir in the lemon juice. Serve the soup warm or cold.

SPINACH SOUP *(page 74)*

Makes about 3¾ cups (900 ml)
1 lb (450 g) spinach, fresh or frozen
1 small onion, chopped
1 tbsp oil
3¾ cups (900 ml) chicken or vegetable stock

1 Wash the spinach thoroughly, or thaw and drain well if frozen.
2 Sauté the onion in the oil to soften.
3 Add the spinach and the stock. Bring to a boil and simmer until tender.
4 Process the mixture until smooth.
5 Decorate with a swirl of yogurt.

LIMA BEAN SOUP *(page 74)*

Makes about 4½ cups (1 liter)
1 tbsp oil
1 onion, chopped
1 carrot, chopped
1 celery stalk, chopped
⅔ cup (100 g) dried lima beans, presoaked
3¾ cups (900 ml) stock or water
1 tbsp tomato juice or paste
1 bay leaf

1 Heat the oil and sauté the onion for about 3 minutes to soften.
2 Add the carrot and celery and cook gently for 3–4 minutes longer.
3 Add the drained lima beans, stock or water, tomato juice or paste, and the bay leaf. Cover and simmer for 1 hour, or cook in a pressure cooker for 20 minutes.
4 Remove the bay leaf and process the mixture until smooth.

FRESH TOMATO SOUP *(page 74)*

Makes about 4½ cups (1 liter)
2 tbsp (25 g) margarine
1 onion, sliced
1 garlic clove, crushed
1 lb (450 g) fresh tomatoes, roughly chopped
2½ cups (600 ml) stock
⅔ cup (150 ml) milk

1 Melt the margarine and sauté the onion and garlic until soft.
2 Add the tomatoes and stock. Cover and simmer for 15 minutes.
3 Remove from the heat and add the milk.
4 Process the mixture until smooth, then strain to remove the tomato skins and seeds, if necessary. Reheat, but do not allow to boil or the soup may curdle.

Soup recipes continued page 76

CHICKEN STOCK SOUP *(page 74)*

Makes about 9 cups (2 liters)

1 chicken carcass or bones from a cooked bird (and giblets, if available)
1 onion, sliced
1 carrot, sliced
1 celery stalk, sliced
1 tsp chopped mixed herbs
1 bay leaf
9 cups (2 liters) water

1 Place the chicken carcass or bones (and giblets), onion, carrot, celery, and herbs in a large saucepan. Add the water and bring to a boil. Skim well, cover, and then simmer for at least 1 hour.
2 Allow the mixture to cool and then strain, discarding the solids.
3 Use as a stock or reheat and serve as it is with small cubes of bread floating on top.
4 For variety and extra flavor, reheat the stock with peas or diced vegetables.
5 To make the soup more substantial, add some cooked rice, barley, noodles, or tiny soup pasta shapes.

CARROT SOUP *(page 74)*

Makes about 4½ cups (1 liter)

1 lb (450 g) carrots, well scrubbed and roughly chopped
2 celery stalks, chopped
2½ cups (600 ml) stock or water
1¼ cups (300 ml) milk

1 Simmer the carrots and celery in the stock or water for about 15 minutes, until the vegetables are soft.
2 Process the mixture until smooth.
3 Add the milk and reheat gently, but do not allow to boil or the soup may curdle.

LENTIL SOUP *(page 74)*

Makes about 6 cups (1½ liters)

1 tbsp oil
1 onion, chopped
2 leeks, chopped
2 carrots, sliced
3 celery stalks, chopped
½ cup (50 g) red or brown lentils (or yellow split peas or barley)
1 tbsp tamari (salt-free soy sauce)
1 tsp cumin seed
4½ cups (1 liter) stock or water

1 Heat the oil and sauté the onion, leeks, carrots, and celery for about 5 minutes, until slightly softened but not browned.
2 Add the lentils, tamari, cumin seed, and water or stock. Bring to a boil, then cover and simmer for about 1 hour, or until the lentils and vegetables are very soft.
3 Process the mixture until smooth.

HOMEMADE HARD BISCUITS *(page 74)*

Ingredients

Thick slices of whole-wheat or white bread (bread that is a few days old is fine)

1 Preheat oven to its lowest setting.
2 Cut the bread into pieces, squares, or triangles. Alternatively, use cookie cutters to cut it into attractive shapes.
3 Place the shapes on an ungreased baking sheet and bake in the oven for about 1 hour, until they are dry, hard, and golden brown. Turn the shapes over after 30 minutes so that they color evenly.
4 Cool thoroughly on a wire rack.
5 Store in an airtight container. The biscuits will keep for several days.

SNACKS AND PICNICS

STICKMAN FEAST

Few children will be able to resist this funny figure or its combination of foods. The head is made from a mild version of the Mexican dip, guacamole. Add some chili sauce, sliced fresh green chilies, or powdered chili for the rest of the family. The dippers can be any selection of scrubbed, sliced fresh vegetables (steam them to soften when serving to children under a year, particularly small pieces such as the carrot features). Pancakes are always popular and can be made in batches for freezing. They're equally good filled with a fruit purée, as shown here, or savory mixtures.

Stickman feast
Arrange bread, vegetables, and cheese for the body and limbs. The head is a generous portion of guacamole. *(Recipe p. 83)*

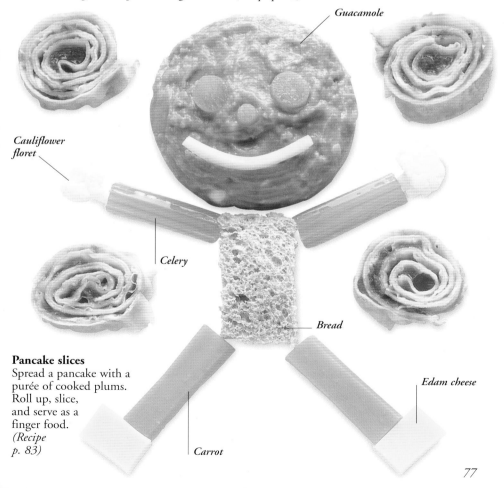

Guacamole

Cauliflower floret

Celery

Bread

Pancake slices
Spread a pancake with a purée of cooked plums. Roll up, slice, and serve as a finger food. *(Recipe p. 83)*

Edam cheese

Carrot

SANDWICH MAN

Don't overlook sandwiches as a quick, easy, and nutritious meal for your child. Thin slices of whole-wheat or other whole grain bread can be shaped with a decorative metal cutter for fun. Top with anything you wish: soft or hard cheeses, grated vegetables and fruits, cooked meats, no-sugar-added jams, or bean purées – the choice is endless. Try not to use lots of butter or margarine: a thin scraping is enough (in fact, your child won't even notice if you don't use any on the sandwiches). Excess use of butter or margarine is an undesirable habit, learned all too often at a very early age.

Sandwich man
Shape a slice of whole-wheat bread with a cookie cutter, spread with a mixture of farmer cheese, chopped dates, and watercress and serve on a bed of shredded lettuce.

Fruity building blocks
Make these from chunky cubes of melon: orange crenshaw and fragrant cantaloupe.

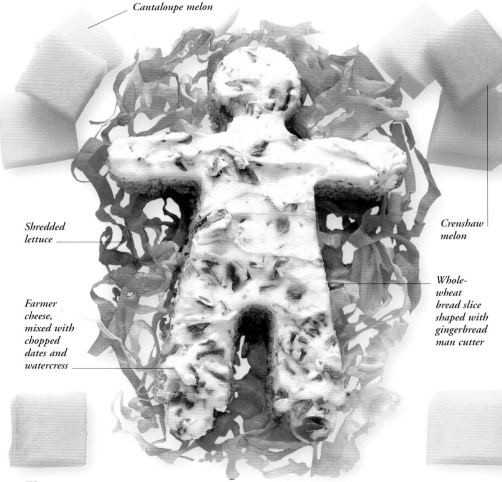

Cantaloupe melon

Shredded lettuce

Crenshaw melon

Farmer cheese, mixed with chopped dates and watercress

Whole-wheat bread slice shaped with gingerbread man cutter

DIP IDEAS

PEANUT BUTTER OR
TAHINI AND SOFT TOFU

LOW-FAT SOFT CHEESE
AND TOMATO PURÉE

COOKED CHICKEN
LIVERS AND
COTTAGE CHEESE

RIPE AVOCADO AND
COTTAGE CHEESE

Interesting and flavorful dips can be
made from a wide variety of savory
and sweet ingredients and are a good
way of getting a fussy eater to try new
tastes. Serve dips with raw or lightly
steamed vegetables, homemade hard
biscuits, or slices of fruit, but expect
young children to dip their fingers in
too. Use these tasty, nutritious dips as
spreads for sandwiches, toppings for
slices of whole-wheat bread, or fillings
for tomatoes, celery stalks, sweet
peppers, or small pastry shells. Your
child will enjoy the experience of
dipping and tasting, and you will find
that the rest of the family is just as
eager to sample these different ideas.

HUMMUS *(recipe p. 83)*

CHOPPED COOKED SPINACH,
FARMER CHEESE, AND
LEMON JUICE

MASHED TUNA AND
FARMER CHEESE

RASPBERRY PURÉE
AND RICOTTA CHEESE

YOGURT, GRATED COCONUT, AND ORANGE JUICE

BAKING

**BANANA
OATMEAL CAKE**
(recipe p. 83)

**PLAIN OAT
CRACKER**
(recipe p. 41)

**WHOLE-
WHEAT SPONGE
CAKE** *(recipe p. 63)*

There is no good reason why children should have any cakes and cookies in their first two years of life. However, outside pressure from playgroups and parties will doubtless encourage the inevitable taste for sweet things. Prepare for this by getting your child used to less sugary cakes and cookies made from unrefined ingredients. For example, substitute the stronger-tasting, dark brown, unrefined sugar with molasses added to cut down on the amount of sugar required in recipes. Add sweeteners like dried fruits and fruit juices when you can (but avoid honey for children under a year). Try to use whole-wheat flour in your baking too.

GRANOLA BAR *(recipe p. 63)*

**WHOLE-WHEAT FRUIT
SCONE WITH YOGURT
AND JAM** *(recipe p. 84)*

CARROT CAKE
(recipe p. 84)

DATE AND NUT CAKE
(recipe p. 84)

**WHOLE-WHEAT SPONGE
WITH CAROB OR COCOA**
(recipe p. 84)

FOOD ON THE MOVE

Most children become restless and bored when strapped into a car seat or taken on a train for any length of time, so it's a good idea to take a variety of snacks for them to eat so you don't have to keep entertaining them. Don't pack messy foods or things that are difficult to hold. Cut sandwiches, small cookies, and pieces of fruit are best when you are on the move, even if it's just to cheer up your child when you are out shopping. Individual pastry shells are another convenient way to package food when you are traveling with children. Little packages of dried fruit, cubes of hard cheese, and raw or lightly steamed vegetable sticks are also good standbys.

Peeled apple slices

Mini sandwiches
Take care not to overfill sandwiches, or they will be messy to eat. Cut into small squares for easy handling.

GRANOLA BAR
(recipe p. 63)

MINI QUICHE
FLOWER
(recipe p. 48)

PICNIC FOODS

The best picnics are full of surprises but are simple to unpack and serve. Slice plain or whole-wheat pita bread and fill the pocket with salad, a homemade spread, or thinly sliced lean meat. Cut the bread into pieces that are easy to handle when you reach your destination. Alternatively, cut a French loaf in half lengthwise, scoop out some of the dough, and fill with a salad or spread. This can be sliced to make instant sandwiches as soon as you arrive. Assorted dips in tiny containers and plastic bags of prepared vegetables and fresh fruit add the variety that makes for the most successful picnics. Don't forget to take along plenty of drinks and water as well as a supply of napkins.

Carrot cake
This lightly spiced cake is sweetened with grated carrots. It has a moist texture and won't collapse into crumbs. *(Recipe p. 84)*

Pita bread sandwich
Pack in the filling so that there's a generous amount and it doesn't fall out. Serve in small pieces that your child can easily hold.

Vegetable sticks
Accompany the cheese and tomato dip with sticks of raw vegetables.

Zucchini

Diluted orange drink
Drinks are a must for picnics and traveling. Mix on the spot.

Celery

Sweet pepper

Carrot

Tomato dip
Pack a dip made from tomato and farmer cheese into a jar that has a tightly fitting lid.

SNACK AND PICNIC RECIPES

GUACAMOLE *(page 77)*

Ingredients

1 ripe avocado, peeled and cubed
1 small onion, very finely chopped
1 tomato, peeled and finely chopped
1 tbsp plain yogurt
juice of 1 lemon

1 Mash the avocado flesh, then combine with the onion, tomato, yogurt, and lemon juice. Mix to blend the ingredients.
2 Cover the dip with plastic wrap and chill well before serving.

PANCAKE SLICES *(page 77)*

Ingredients for about 8 pancakes

1 cup (100 g) flour
1 egg
1¼ cups (300 ml) milk
2 tbsp oil
puréed cooked fruit such as plum

1 Sift the flour into a bowl.
2 Make a well in the center and crack the egg into it. Gradually mix in the milk by stirring from the center and drawing the dry ingredients into the egg and milk.
3 Heat an omelet pan and brush with a few drops of oil.
4 Pour in enough batter to coat the bottom of the pan. Cook for 1–2 minutes, until the underside of the pancake is golden (keep shaking the pan so the pancake remains loose). Turn with a spatula and cook the other side until golden, 1–2 minutes.
5 If cooking for the family, stack the pancakes as you make them, with a sheet of waxed paper between each one. Keep warm in a low oven.
6 Spread the pancakes with fruit purée, roll up, and slice before serving.

HUMMUS *(page 79)*

Ingredients

½ cup (150 g) chickpeas, presoaked
1 garlic clove, crushed
1 tsp ground cumin
4 tbsp tahini (sesame paste)
4 tbsp lemon juice
1 tbsp water, if necessary

1 Boil the chickpeas in fresh water until soft (1–1½ hours), or cook in a pressure cooker for 30 minutes. Drain and cool.
2 Process the cooked chickpeas with the garlic, cumin, tahini, and lemon juice.
3 Moisten with a little water if needed (it should be the consistency of mayonnaise).

BANANA OATMEAL CAKE *(page 80)*

Ingredients for 1 large cake

¾ cup (75 g) rolled oats
1 cup (225 ml) milk
2½ cups (275 g) flour
¼ cup (50 g) sugar
5 tsp baking powder
2 tsp baking soda
1 tsp ground cinnamon
1 tsp ground nutmeg
¼ cup (50 ml) safflower oil
2 eggs, beaten
2 tsp pure vanilla extract
4–5 bananas, mashed

1 Preheat oven to 350°F (180°C).
2 Combine the oats and milk. Set aside.
3 Mix the dry ingredients.
4 Add the oil, eggs, vanilla, and bananas to the oats and milk. Mix with the dry ingredients until they are just moistened.
5 Fill a greased loaf pan and bake for about 1½ hours. Or fill fluted paper cups and bake for about 35 minutes, or until golden brown. Cool on a wire rack. This cake is best after 2–3 days.

Snack and picnic recipes continued page 84

WHOLE-WHEAT SCONES WITH FRUIT OR CHEESE *(page 80)*

Ingredients for about 10 scones
4 tbsp (50 g) butter or margarine
2 cups (225 g) whole-wheat flour, sifted
* with 1 tbsp baking powder*
¼ cup (50 g) dried fruit or grated cheese
⅔ cup (150 ml) milk

1 Preheat oven to 450°F (250°C).
2 Rub the butter or margarine into the flour and baking powder until the mixture resembles fine bread crumbs.
3 Add the dried fruit or grated cheese, then gradually stir in the milk.
4 Turn the dough onto a floured surface and knead lightly to remove any cracks.
5 Roll out to about ¾ in (2 cm) thick.
6 Cut into shapes with a small cookie cutter and place on a greased baking sheet. Use the trimmings to make more scones.
7 Bake for about 10 minutes, until well risen and golden brown.

WHOLE-WHEAT SPONGE CAKE *(page 80)*

Ingredients
¼ lb (100 g) soft margarine
½ cup (100 g) sugar
2 eggs, beaten
1 cup (100 g) whole-wheat flour, sifted
* with 1½ tsp baking powder*
1 tbsp carob or cocoa powder

1 Preheat oven to 350°F (180°C).
2 Line one 8 in (20 cm) loaf pan with waxed paper.
3 Cream the fat and sugar together.
4 Mix in the eggs and flour, keeping the mixture smooth.
5 Divide the mixture in two and mix the carob or cocoa powder into one half.
6 Place alternate spoonfuls of the mixtures in the pan. Swirl with a knife several times to create a marbled effect.
7 Bake for 15–20 minutes, until firm. Turn out onto a wire rack to cool.

CARROT CAKE *(page 80)*

Ingredients
⅔ cup (150 ml) oil
½ cup (100 g) sugar
3 eggs, beaten
1 cup (200 g) flour
2 tsp baking soda
1½ tsp ground cinnamon
4–5 large carrots, peeled and grated

1 Preheat oven to 300°F (150°C).
2 Grease a 9 x 13 in (23 x 32 cm) pan and line it with greased waxed paper.
3 Beat the oil into the sugar.
4 Add the eggs and beat well to mix.
5 Sift all the dry ingredients together and add to the wet mixture. Mix well.
6 Fold in the grated carrots.
7 Spoon the mixture into the pan and bake for about 1 hour, until golden brown.

DATE AND NUT CAKE *(page 80)*

Ingredients
2 cups (350 g) dried dates, chopped
1 cup (225 ml) boiling water
2½ cups (275 g) flour
1 tsp baking powder
1 tsp baking soda
¼ cup (50 g) sugar
½ cup (65 g) nuts, finely chopped
⅓ cup (75 ml) oil
1 egg, beaten
1 tsp pure vanilla extract

1 Preheat oven to 350°F (180°C).
2 Grease and line a loaf pan.
3 Place dates in a bowl and pour over the boiling water. Stir and cool.
4 Mix the flour, baking powder, baking soda, sugar, and nuts.
5 Stir the oil, egg, and vanilla into the cooled date mixture.
6 Add the wet mixture to the dry ingredients, stirring just to moisten them.
7 Spoon into the pan and bake for about 1 hour. Or fill fluted paper cups and bake for about 30 minutes, until golden brown.

3

SPECIAL OCCASIONS

As long as your child is eating and enjoying a healthy diet most of the time, there is no reason to exclude treats on birthdays, holidays, and festive occasions. You can start early to develop good habits by encouraging your child to appreciate healthier treats than the commercial cakes, cookies, and candies that are usually offered at such times. Experiment with carob instead of chocolate, bake with wholesome ingredients, and offer fresh and dried fruits instead of sugar-laden and artificially colored candy. Healthy habits learned early will last a lifetime.

EASTER FEAST

Easter shouldn't be solely about Easter eggs. You can make it a special occasion with other festive foods and shapes, such as those shown here. Even older children will be excited by this Easter bunny, which should divert their attention from the ubiquitous chocolate eggs. The open sandwich is topped with grated apple, carrot, and hard cheese mixed with yogurt and mayonnaise. Raisins and carrots provide the finishing touches. Make the egg by rolling a teaspoon of farmer cheese between the palms of your hands. You can decorate it with chopped fresh parsley or ground nuts.

Easter bunny
Serve an appetizing spread of grated apple, carrot, cheese, yogurt, and mayonnaise on French bread, with raisins for the bunny's eyes and carrot pieces for its whiskers and ears.

Fruity chick with nest
This chirpy Easter chick is made of soaked dried apricot halves and pieces of fresh pineapple. A farmer cheese egg sits in a carrot, cucumber, and zucchini nest.

Shaped raw carrot

Soaked dried apricot

Raisin

French bread

Fresh pineapple

Carrot, cucumber, and zucchini nest

Farmer cheese

EASTER TREATS

Start early to develop good habits where chocolate is concerned, particularly at Easter, when there is so much of it around. Make this a time for special treats, but follow the ideas shown here to help cut down on the chocolate intake. Rather than offering pieces of solid chocolate, give your child fruit or cereal cookies that have been dipped in melted chocolate. Or try using a carob bar instead of chocolate: your child might like the taste and it contains less saturated fat and refined sugar.

FARMER CHEESE EGGS DUSTED WITH COCOA

DRIED APRICOT DIPPED IN CHOCOLATE

GRAPES DIPPED IN MELTED CHOCOLATE

CAROB BISCUIT *(recipe p. 92)*

PEANUT BUTTER BALLS *(recipe p. 92)*

FRUIT TART *(recipe p. 73)*

CAROB-DIPPED STRAWBERRY

CHOCOLATE-DIPPED GRANOLA BAR *(recipe p. 63)*

CHOCOLATE-DIPPED OATMEAL COOKIE *(recipe p. 62)*

ICED YOGURT EGG *(recipe p. 92)*

CHRISTMAS DINNER

Your child should share in the traditional Christmas dinner your family enjoys, but perhaps you can include one or two special items that can be prepared in advance, like this frozen yogurt snowman. Since Christmas dinner tends to be a feast of rich, hearty foods, give your child small portions. Children are usually excited by the festive atmosphere and the decorations and may not have much of an appetite. Arrange their food enticingly in morsels so they can feed themselves. You will have more time to relax with the family and enjoy your meal.

Frozen yogurt snowman
Use soaked dried apricots and golden raisins to give the snowman colorful features. *(Recipe p. 92)*

Christmas star
Arrange turkey breast, roast potatoes, carrot strips, and quartered brussels sprouts into a traditional shape.

MINI MINCEMEAT
TART

Roast
potato

Brussels
sprouts in
bite-size
pieces

CHRISTMAS
STAR

Steamed carrot strip

Turkey breast

CHRISTMAS TREATS

GINGERBREAD
SANTA CLAUS
(recipe p. 92)

For the Christmas holiday, prepare healthy treats in advance and freeze or store them in airtight containers. A variety of tempting goodies can be made to replace the traditionally rich, high-fat, sugary Christmas fare. Invest in some seasonal cookie cutters so that you can create festive and appealing shapes like this angel and bell. Try to use small pieces of fresh fruits in pies to give them extra color, and tone down rich mincemeat by adding chopped fresh apple or grated carrot to the fruit mixture before you fill and bake the pies in the oven.

GINGERBREAD
ANGEL
(recipe p. 92)

WHOLE-WHEAT
ALMOND COOKIE
(recipe p. 92)

OATMEAL
COOKIE
(recipe p. 62)

SHORTBREAD
(recipe p. 93)

MINCEMEAT PIE WITH APPLE

WHOLE-WHEAT FRUIT
PIE *(recipe p. 73)*

MINI PALMIERS *(recipe p. 93)*

DATE WITH RICOTTA CHEESE

BIRTHDAY PARTY

As long as children enjoy a healthy diet most of the time, there is no reason to exclude special treats on their birthdays and on other festive occasions. They may even come to associate such treats with special occasions only, and not demand or expect them every week. The most important thing about party food is its presentation. Most children are too excited to eat much, and you will want to cut down on your preparation time. So select a limited menu carefully and incorporate good healthy food wherever you can.

Birthday cake
For a nutritious and appetizing cake, follow one of the recipes and decorate with a topping of cream cheese, natural yogurt, and grated orange peel. *(Recipes pp. 63, 83, and 84)*

Finger salad
Fill a paper cupcake liner with grated carrot, apple, and beets. Decorate with a cherry tomato.

Tower sandwich
Layer whole-wheat and white bread with sliced tomato, alfalfa sprouts, farmer cheese, and chicken liver pâté. Serve in pieces.

Open sandwich
To make these eye-catching and mouthwatering morsels, top small pieces of bread with fresh vegetables and firm cheese.

OPEN
SANDWICH

Mini quiche
Line tiny pie pans with pastry and fill them with a tasty custard made of eggs and cheese for this mini quiche in the shape of a narrow boat. *(Recipe p. 48)*

BOAT-SHAPED
QUICHE

MINI DATE AND NUT
CAKE *(recipe p. 84)*

Gingerbread figure
Cut to resemble little men, these cookies are universally popular and store well in an airtight tin. Decorate with dried fruit before baking. *(Recipe p. 93)*

Fruit mousse
A dollop of thick yogurt decorates this dessert, made of unsweetened grape (or other fruit) juice, puréed fresh fruit, and natural yogurt. *(Recipe p. 63)*

Yogurt

Raspberry and yogurt mousse set in a heart-shaped mold

CANDY AND OTHER TREATS

To forbid sweet treats entirely is unrealistic. Allowing children unlimited amounts is also wrong. When babies are young, you won't have any problems, but as children grow older, they'll inevitably meet others who eat such things without thinking. Try to be prepared for this by encouraging your child to appreciate healthier foods and to accept sweet rationing and routines. A sweet with meals is less destructive on new teeth than having sweet snacks throughout the day. Get your child into the habit of brushing his teeth after every meal, and make it fun rather than a chore.

APRICOT AND ORANGE
BALL *(recipe p. 93)*

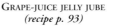

ORANGE JELLY JUBE *(recipe p. 93)*

GRAPE-JUICE JELLY JUBE
(recipe p. 93)

DATE CRUNCHY
(recipe p. 93)

SPECIAL OCCASIONS RECIPES

CAROB COOKIES *(page 87)*

Ingredients for 15–20 cookies
¼ lb (100 g) butter or margarine
¼ cup (50 g) sugar
½ tsp pure vanilla extract
½ cup (100 g) flour, less 2 tbsp
2 tbsp carob powder

1 Preheat oven to 375°F (190°C).
2 Cream the butter or margarine and sugar together until light and fluffy. Mix in the vanilla extract.
3 Sift the flour with the carob powder and stir into the fat and sugar mixture.
4 Drop teaspoons of the mixture, well apart, onto a greased baking sheet. Or chill the mixture to firm slightly, roll out, and shape with small cookie cutters. Bake the cookies for 10–15 minutes, until hard.

PEANUT BUTTER BALLS *(page 87)*

Ingredients for about 15 pieces
½ cup (100 g) smooth peanut butter
⅓ cup (50 g) raisins
1 cup (175 g) wheatgerm
¼ cup (40 g) dried milk powder
¼ cup (25 g) ground nuts

1 Mix all the ingredients together and roll into balls or egg shapes.
2 Store in the refrigerator to help them stay firm and keep their shape.

ICED YOGURT EGG *(page 87)*

Ingredients
1½ cups (350 ml) plain yogurt
¾ cup (175 ml) orange juice
1 tsp grated orange peel

1 Mix all the ingredients together well.
2 Pour into a suitable container or into shaped containers for freezing.
3 Freeze until solid.
4 Use this recipe also for the Frozen yogurt snowman (see p. 88).

WHOLE-WHEAT ALMOND COOKIES *(page 89)*

Ingredients for 15–20 cookies
12 tbsp (175 g) butter or margarine
1 cup (100 g) sugar
1 egg, beaten
½ cup (100 g) whole-wheat flour
½ cup (50 g) ground almonds

1 Preheat oven to 350°F (180°C).
2 Cream the butter or margarine and sugar until light and fluffy.
3 Gradually mix in the egg.
4 Fold in the flour and ground almonds and mix well.
5 Spoon the mixture in small dollops, set close together to form circles, onto a well-greased baking sheet. Bake the cookies for 10–15 minutes, until lightly browned.

MINI PALMIERS *(page 89)*

Ingredients for 16 pieces
8 oz (225 g) frozen puff pastry, thawed
3 tbsp good-quality strawberry jam with a high proportion of fruit

1 Preheat oven to 425°F (220°C).
2 Roll out the pastry on a floured surface into a long rectangle ¼ in (6 mm) thick.
3 Thinly spread the whole pastry rectangle with 2 tbsp of the jam.
4 Fold the long edges of the pastry in to meet at the center and spread with the remaining jam. Fold the pastry in half lengthwise to hide the folds and form a narrow strip.
5 Press the pastry down with your hand and cut into ¼ in (6 mm) slices with a sharp knife.
6 Place the slices on a dampened baking sheet, cut sides down and well apart to allow the cookies to spread.
7 Bake near the top of the oven for 10 minutes. Turn over and bake for 3–4 minutes longer, until golden brown.

WHOLE-WHEAT SHORTBREAD
(page 89)

Ingredients for 10–15 pieces
10 tbsp (150 g) butter or margarine
1⅔ cups (175 g) whole-wheat flour
⅓ cup (50 g) rice flour
¼ cup (50 g) sugar

1 Preheat oven to 325°F (160°C).
2 Beat the butter until thoroughly soft, then gradually work in the dry ingredients to make a stiff dough, using your hand or a wooden spoon.
3 Place the dough on a floured surface and knead lightly. Roll out to a thickness of about ¼ in (6 mm).
4 Cut into shapes or slices and place on a greased baking sheet. Bake the cookies for about 30 minutes, until tinged brown.

GINGERBREAD COOKIES
(pages 89 and 91)

Ingredients for 15–20 cookies
3 cups (350 g) flour
1 tsp baking soda
2 tsp ground ginger
¼ lb (100 g) butter or margarine
1 cup (100 g) sugar
3 tbsp (45 ml) molasses
1 egg, beaten

1 Preheat oven to 375°F (190°C).
2 Sift the flour, baking soda, and ginger together. Rub in the butter or margarine until the mixture resembles fine bread crumbs. Stir in the sugar.
3 Warm the molasses until it is easy to pour. Make a well in the center of the dry ingredients and add the molasses with the egg. Mix until well blended.
4 Turn the dough out onto a lightly floured board and knead lightly. Roll out to a thickness of about ¼ in (6 mm).
5 Cut out shapes and place, well apart to allow for spreading, on a lightly greased baking sheet. Bake for about 10 minutes, until golden brown.

APRICOT AND ORANGE BALLS
(page 91)

Ingredients for about 24 pieces
1 lb (450 g) dried apricots, chopped
1 medium orange, peeled and chopped
1 cup (65 g) grated coconut
½ cup (65 g) ground nuts

1 Mix all the ingredients together (mince them in a food processor, if possible).
2 Shape into balls and chill until firm.

JELLY JUBES *(page 91)*

Ingredients for about 20 pieces
1½ cups (350 ml) unsweetened fruit juice
4 envelopes unflavored gelatin or
*   vegetarian substitute such as agar-agar*
2 tsp lemon juice

1 Heat the fruit juice but do not boil.
2 Dissolve the gelatin in a bowl standing over a saucepan of boiling water. Stir constantly until dissolved.
3 Stir the gelatin into the fruit juice and mix well. Remove from the heat and add the lemon juice.
4 Pour into a pan ½–1 in (10–20 mm) deep or into individual molds. Let stand until firm. Cut the jelly in the pan into shapes, if desired. Store in the refrigerator.

DATE CRUNCHIES *(page 91)*

Ingredients for about 20 pieces
¼ lb (100 g) butter or margarine
½ cup (75 g) chopped, pitted, dried dates
½ cup (75 g) dark brown sugar
1–1½ cups (100–150 g) sugar-free
*   whole-wheat breakfast cereal*
shredded coconut (optional)

1 Mix the butter, dates, and sugar in a saucepan and cook over low heat until the dates have softened.
2 Remove from the heat and mix in the breakfast cereal to make a stiff consistency.
3 Cool, then shape into balls.
4 Roll in coconut to decorate, if desired.

INDEX

J, K, L

jelly: fruit jelly car, 64, 72
  jelly jubes, 91, 93
kitchen equipment, 11
lactose intolerance, 25
leafy package train, 68, 72–73
legumes, 14–15, 66
lentils: cheesy monster, 44, 48
  lentil soup, 76
lima bean soup, 75

M, N

mealtimes, 22–23
meat, 14–15, 54–63
meatloaf car, 58, 62
meatball pony, 57
menus, 18, 21
messy eaters, 20–21
milk, 24
  lactose intolerance, 25
  nutrition, 26–27
  snacks, 29
  weaning, 12, 16
minerals, 28
mini palmiers, 89, 93
mini sandwiches, 81
mouse, pear, 43
mousse, fruit, 59, 63
nutrition, 26–29
nuts, 14–15, 20

O

oatmeal: banana oatmeal cake,
    80, 83
  granola bar tree, 60, 63
  merry meatball pony, 57, 62
  oatmeal cookie dessert, 57,
    62
  plain oat crackers, 41
omelet, cat-face, 43, 48
overweight children, 24

P

palmiers, mini, 89, 93
pancakes: breakfast, 41
  slices, 77, 83
pasta boat, pick-up, 61, 63
pastry, 54

peanut butter balls, 87, 92
pears: butterfly pastie, 51, 53
  pear mouse, 43
peas: fresh pea soup, 75
pick-up pasta boat, 61, 63
picnics, 82
pioneer log cabin, 60
pizza, smiley face, 46, 48
polka-dot octopus, 67
pony, meatball, 57
potatoes: tasty teddy bear, 56,
    62
  tuna potato boat, 52
processed foods, 31
protein, 17, 20, 26, 28
purées, 31

Q, R

quiche flower, 47, 48
rattle munch, 59, 63
refusal to eat, 25
reheating food, 30
restaurants, 23
rewards, 22
rice: rattle munch, 59, 63
rocket, vegetable, 69, 73

S

safety, food preparation,
    30–31
salt, 7, 27, 36
sandwiches: mini sandwiches,
    81
  sandwich man, 78
savory cone, 71, 73
scones, whole-wheat, 80, 84
seeds, 14–15
self-feeding, 17
shortbread, whole-wheat, 89,
    93
shrimp, jumping, 51
smiley-face pizza, 46, 48
smoked haddock: funny fish,
    49, 53
snacks, 23, 25, 77–84
  planning, 29
soups, 74–76
spinach soup, 75
spoonfeeding, 12
stickman feast, 77, 83

stir-fried kite, 70
storing food, 30
sugar, 27
sunshine breakfast, 40

T

tart, mixed fruit, 69, 73
teething, 19
tell-the-time breakfast, 39
toddlers, 20–21
tomatoes: fresh tomato soup,
    75
  smiley-face pizza, 46, 48
training cup, 11, 16
treats, 22, 87, 89, 91
tuna potato boat, 52
turkey: tasty teddy bear, 56,
    62
turnovers: butterfly turnover,
    51, 53
  crab turnover, 54

U, V

utensils, 11
vegetables, 20, 32–33
  food pyramid, 26
  introducing, 14–15
  leafy package train, 68,
    72–73
  nutrients, 28
  preparation, 31
  recipes, 64–73
  savory cone, 71, 73
  self-feeding, 17
  soups, 74–76
vegetarian diet, 13
vitamins, 28

W, Y

weaning, 12–15
whole-wheat almond cookies,
    89, 92
whole-wheat bread, 41
whole-wheat pie, 73, 89
whole-wheat shortbread, 89,
    93
whole-wheat sponge, 58, 63
  with carob or cocoa, 80, 84
yogurt egg, iced, 87, 92

ACKNOWLEDGMENTS

The publisher would like to thank the
following individuals for their contribution
to this book.

PHOTOGRAPHY
Photographs by Martin Brigdale, pages 37–91.
All other photographs by Jules Selmes except
Dave King, pages 10–11

HOME ECONOMISTS
Dolly Meers, Janice Murfitt

NUTRITION CONSULTANT
Karen Gunner

ADDITIONAL EDITORIAL AND
DESIGN ASSISTANCE
Nicky Adamson, Claire Cross, Caroline Greene,
Barbara Minton, Maureen Rissik

INDEX
Hilary Bird

TEXT FILM
The Brightside Partnership, London